# FESTIVE FOLDING

★ ★ ★ ★ ★

# FESTIVE FOLDING

★ ★ ★ ★ ★

## Decorative origami for parties and celebrations

PAUL JACKSON

NEW
BURLINGTON
BOOKS

**A QUINTET BOOK**

Published by New Burlington Books
6 Blundell Street
London N7 9BH

ISBN 1–85348–338–9

This book was designed and produced by
Quintet Publishing Limited
6 Blundell Street
London N7 9BH

Creative Director: Terry Jeavons
Designer: Stuart Walden
Project Editor: Judith Simons
Editor: Henrietta Wilkinson
Illustrator: David Kemp
Photographer: Paul Forrester

Typeset in Great Britain by
Central Southern Typesetters, Eastbourne
Manufactured in Singapore by
Chroma Graphics (Overseas) Pte Ltd, (Singapore)
Printed in Singapore by Kim Hup Lee Printing Co. Pte. Ltd.

# CONTENTS

# INTRODUCTION

★ ★ ★ ★ ★

# FOREWORD

**W**hy do people fold paper? Most do so because they enjoy making something out of nothing. A sheet of paper is so ordinary to us that to transform it into a beautiful object can seem miraculous. But another reason is its simplicity. Folding paper needs no tools, no specialist equipment, no machinery – just the paper and your hands. It is relaxing, involving, and immensely rewarding.

The first papers capable of being folded were made in China about 2,000 years ago, although there is no evidence that the Chinese folded paper in a decorative way at that time. A few dozen ancient Japanese designs have survived into the modern era, but since the secret of making paper did not actually cross to Japan until several centuries after its invention in China, the exact origins of the craft are obscure.

Traditional Japanese designs have been the inspiration for the recent flood of new creative work from Japan and the West, and the Japanese word for paper folding – origami – has been adopted worldwide. Today, there are many thousands of designs in an astonishing range of styles and techniques. What must have once seemed a trivial diversion has proven to be a craft, or art, of extraordinary richness. There are now societies of paper folders in most major Western countries who organize exhibitions and courses, and publish a growing number of high-quality specialist publications. Origami has come of age.

Please read the next few pages before attempting any of the designs. They will give you all the information you need to understand the instructions for the projects and to choose the right papers.

Good luck and happy festive folding!

# PAPER

**M**ost types of paper are suitable for folding, but the trick behind successful folding is matching the right paper to the right design. Avoid using papers that do not crease sharply, such as newspaper, tissue or paper towels, unless these are particularly specified.

Specialist Japanese shops usually sell square origami paper in packets, but these outlets are few and far between, and local art and craft suppliers do not always sell it. In any case, origami paper is often expensive and the colours can be harsh, although having different colours or designs on the two sides can be very useful for certain projects.

Good papers for trying out a design include typing paper, writing paper, photocopy paper and computer paper. These are all inexpensive, easily available and crease very well. If nothing else is around, a page cut from a glossy magazine will also fold well.

When folding a design for a festive occasion, a special paper will always make a design look more attractive. Special papers may be bought from two main sources: shops which supply materials to artists, and those which supply materials to graphic artists and designers. Large cities sometimes have shops which specialize in selling paper, but they are disappointingly few in number. Patterned giftwrap paper, sold by stationers, is useful for decorative designs.

In the case of designs which need to be sturdy, such as the Easter *Egg Basket*, use thick artist's papers which can absorb moisture without warping, such as Ingres paper or watercolour paper. This will allow you to employ the so-called 'wet folding' process: before folding a suitable paper, stroke both sides with a lightly dampened – not wet – cloth, then fold; the paper will dry rigid into its folded shape. Even the thickest watercolour paper becomes pliable when wet and will fold into a design of remarkable strength. Other papers, such as drawing paper or thin card, are suitable for general folding but are not suitable for this 'wet folding' process, because they warp and shred when wet.

Some of the designs, such as the *Witch on a Broomstick* are best made from a sheet which has different colours on its two sides. If you cannot find such papers, use two thin sheets of different colours and fold them, back-to-back, as one layer.

Stationers often sell sheets or rolls of metallic foil backed with paper. This material is very malleable for folding, but has a harsh, crude surface which can look rather unattractive. Use it selectively, perhaps for festive decorations such as the *Bauble* or the *Bell*. To soften the reflective surface but to keep the folding properties of foil, try covering the foil-side with a layer of soft-coloured tissue. The effect can be very beautiful.

The introductory paragraphs to each design suggest what weight of paper to use. Lightweight paper is the weight of typing paper, computer paper or lighter papers, such as airmail paper. Mediumweight paper is the weight of drawing paper. Heavy paper is the weight of watercolour paper. It is advisable to use the weight suggested, but it is only a guide. A paper of another weight may work equally well, so feel free to experiment.

④

③

① Square sheets of paper printed with traditional Japanese motifs on one side and left white on the reverse; available from Oriental gift shops.

② Printing paper in plain colours.

③ Square sheets of 'duo' origami paper, printed with different contrasting or harmonizing colours on each side; available in packets.

④ Machine-made marbled paper, sold commercially as 'elephant hide'.

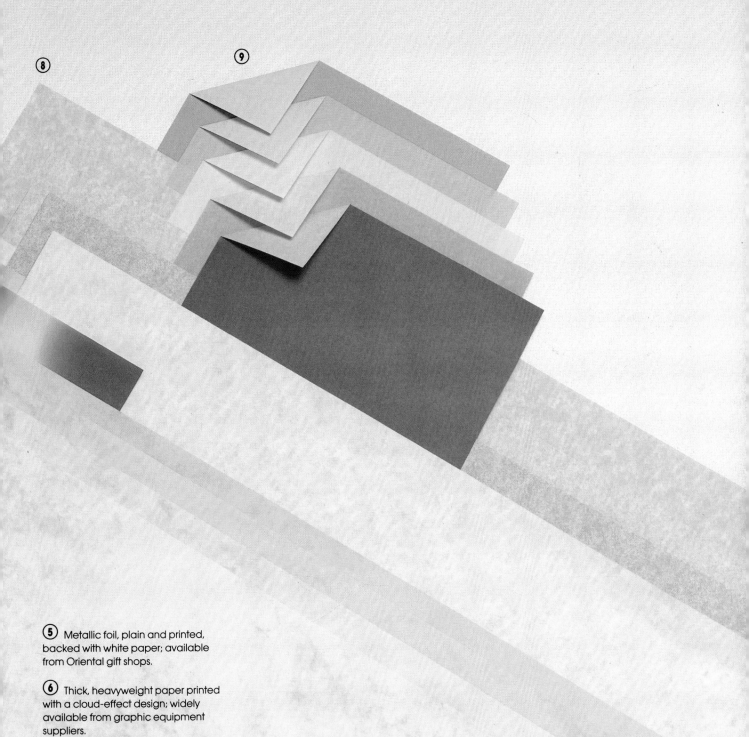

**⑤** Metallic foil, plain and printed, backed with white paper; available from Oriental gift shops.

**⑥** Thick, heavyweight paper printed with a cloud-effect design; widely available from graphic equipment suppliers.

**⑦** Origami paper in plain colours printed with white bands down the centre of each sheet; suitable for decorations.

**⑧** Thick, heavyweight paper printed with a mottled design; widely available from graphic equipment suppliers.

**⑨** Traditional square origami paper, printed in plain colours on one side and left white on the reverse.

# SYMBOLS

Refer to this table when
folding. Make sure that you
follow all the symbols on all
the steps

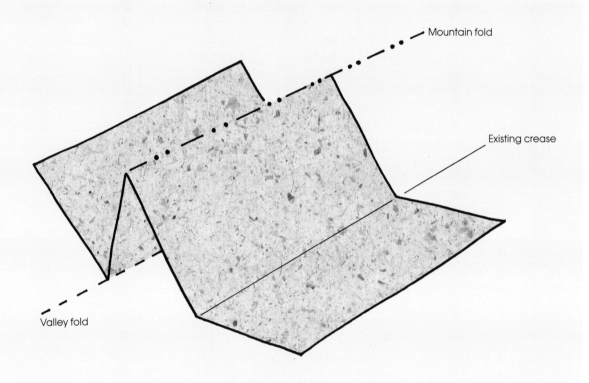

Mountain fold

Existing crease

Valley fold

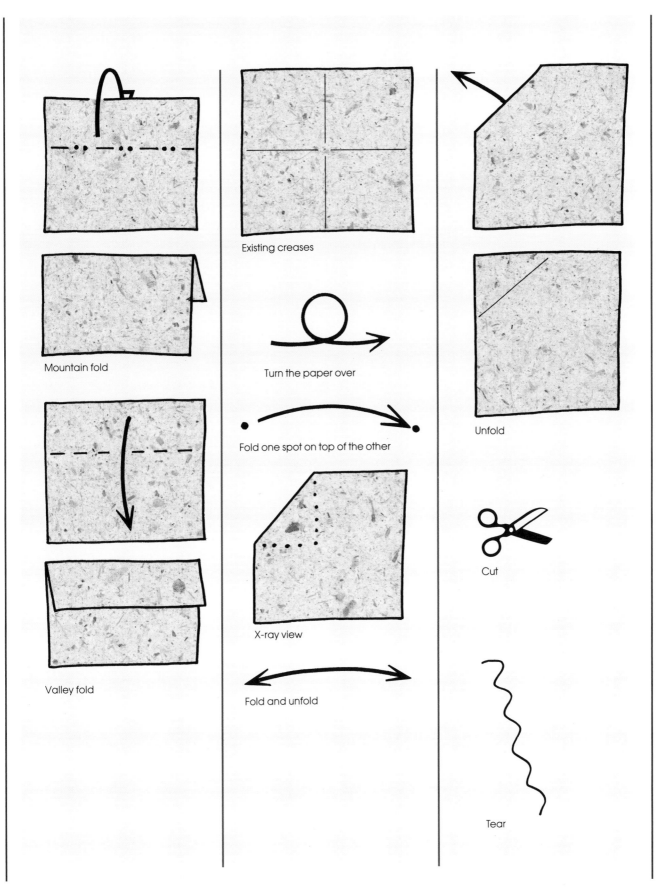

Mountain fold

Valley fold

Existing creases

Turn the paper over

Fold one spot on top of the other

X-ray view

Fold and unfold

Unfold

Cut

Tear

# TIPS ON FOLDING

**F**olding paper is not difficult, but it can become difficult if you fold in an incorrect way. To help you fold properly, here are some tips:

● Fold against a hard, level surface such as a table top or hardback book. Experts fold entirely in the air, but this is awkward for beginners. Nevertheless, there will be occasions, particularly when folding the last stages of a design, when you will need to pick up the paper and fold it in the air, but do so only when necessary.

● Fold slowly, do not rush! Folding needs to be done carefully and neatly. A few sloppy creases here and there can throw everything else out of alignment, so check and double-check the accuracy of your folds.

● Fold crisply and firmly.

● Look at the diagrams and read all the instructions. All too often mistakes are made by looking at one without reference to the other. Look at *all* the symbols (see pages 14 and 15) on a step, checking whether a crease is a valley or a mountain, which corner or edge is at the top of the paper, whether you should turn the paper over, how the lettered corners move about from step to step, and so on.

● The symbols and written instructions for each step will make a shape which looks like the next illustration. So it is important to keep looking ahead to the next diagram to see what shape you are trying to make. Never look at one step in isolation from the others, but look ahead, then back, then ahead and so on.

● Before folding a design, check that the paper you are using is *exactly* square, *exactly* a 2 × 1 rectangle, or whatever the shape specified, and that it is not too small, too large, too thick or too thin for that design.

● Wash your hands!

---

**STAR RATING**

To help you judge the difficulty of a design, a graded star rating has been included with each project.

★ elementary
★★ fairly simple
★★★ not too difficult
★★★★ fairly difficult

# FOLDING
# TECHNIQUES

It is a simple matter to make a valley or mountain crease, but techniques become more complex when more than one crease is made at a time, such as when a corner or edge is opened out and pushed into itself. This procedure is known as either the 'inside reverse fold' (commonly known simply as the 'reverse fold.'), or its opposite, the 'outside reverse fold'. Before folding a design which contains this procedure, try it out a few times first by folding the examples below.

## INSIDE REVERSE FOLDS

**1** Using an oblong scrap of paper, fold the paper in half.

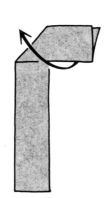

**3** Unfold . . .

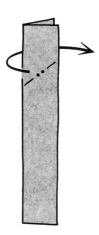

**5** Mountain fold along the line of the valley fold, making a flexible crease.

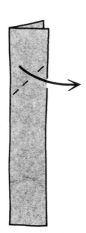

**2** Valley fold as shown.

**4** . . . like this.

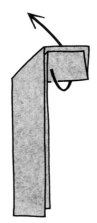

**6** Unfold.

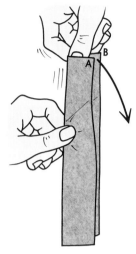

**7** Hold the paper as shown, thumb inside the paper between A and B. Move the top hand down and to the right . . .

**8** . . . separating A from B and making mountain and valley folds as shown, collapsing the paper . . .

**9** . . . like this.

**10** The inside reverse fold complete.

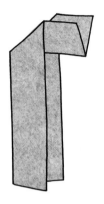

**11** This diagram denotes an inside reverse fold.

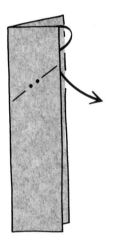

**12** Reverse folds can be at any angle, such as this . . .

**13** . . . which is almost folded in half.

**14** This is a small reverse fold, in which a corner is pushed in . . .

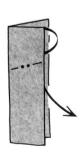

**15** . . . like this. Practise these reverse folds.

# OUTSIDE REVERSE FOLDS

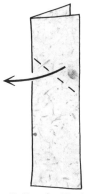

**1** Start with Step 2 of the inside reverse fold, then valley fold as shown.

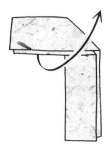

**2** Unfold . . .

**3** . . . like this.

**4** Mountain fold along the line of the valley fold, making a flexible crease.

**5** Unfold.

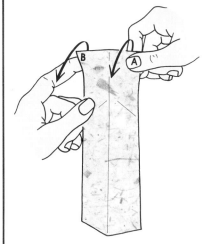

**6** Hold carefully as shown. With the left thumb, push into the paper at the top of the V-shaped crease, while pulling edge BA towards you . . .

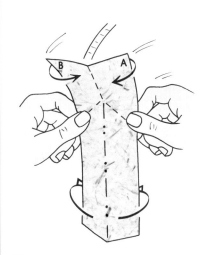

**7** . . . like this. Crease mountains and valleys as shown. Bring edge BA to the front while moving the hands backwards . . .

**8** . . . like this. Collapse further.

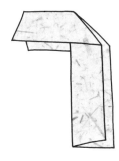

**9** The outside reverse fold complete.

**10** This diagram denotes an outside reverse fold.

# 1

# CHRISTMAS

★ ★ ★ ★ ★

# SIX-POINTED STAR

*TRADITIONAL*

**O**ne of the simplest and most attractive of all folded decorations, the six-pointed star uses the most basic folding techniques. Steps 1–4 show how to make an equilateral triangle (one with all its sides of equal length) from a square. If you know another method of doing this by all means use it, although the one shown here is accurate and pleasing.

Make several stars, in an array of bright colours, and hang from the Christmas tree for extra sparkle.

**STAR RATING ★★**

**PAPERS**

Use a square of paper of any weight or size. The best paper to use for this decoration is paper-backed metallic foil, which reflects the light and will make the star stand out against the dark foliage of a natural Christmas tree.

**OTHER EQUIPMENT**

Scissors; needle and thread.

**1** Fold in half, left to right.

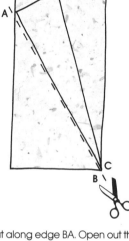

**3** Cut along edge BA. Open out the bottom left-hand triangle and discard the remainder of the paper. Add creases which run into corners B and C to locate the centre of the triangle.

**2** Turn in the top layer corner to exactly touch the crease made in Step 1, at such a point that the new crease will run exactly down to the bottom corner. Take your time lining it up – this is the most important crease in the whole design. Badly placed, it will spoil the shape of the star.

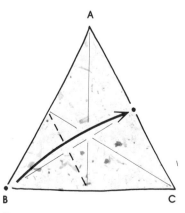

**4** Fold B across to the opposite edge.

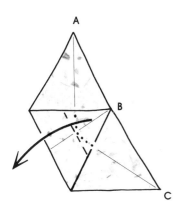

**5** Fold B back along a crease which passes over the centre of the triangle.

**7** Repeat Steps 4 and 5 with A. Tuck the left-hand part of the pleat under B to lock A, B and C together in a symmetrical pattern.

**9** The Six-Pointed Star complete. To suspend, attach a loop to the star with needle and thread. The star looks most effective when hung in groups.

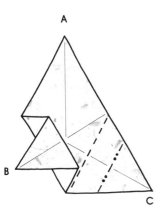

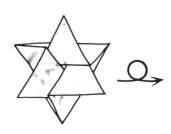

**6** Repeat Steps 4 and 5 with C.

**8** Like this. Turn over.

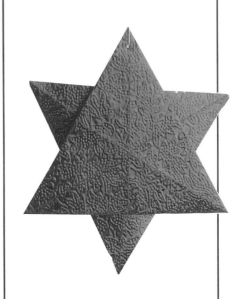

# BAUBLE

*ORIGIN UNKNOWN*

**H**ere is another stunning decoration for the Christmas tree. This may seem like a complex design, but it is little more than a simple crease pattern repeated many times along the paper. The secret of success is to crease with care and accuracy.

**1** With the paper right side up, valley fold twice to form three equal sections.

**2** Make valley creases midway between each section, creating six equal divisions.

**3** Make valley creases midway between the existing creases, creating 12 equal divisions.

**4** Make valley creases midway between each of the existing creases, creating 24 equal divisions. Keep the folds accurate.

**5** Fold the sheet in half along its length. Unfold.

**6** Fold the sides into the middle of the sheet, creasing right along its length. Unfold.

**7** Look at the crease pattern so far. All the existing creases are valleys, the new ones will be mountains.

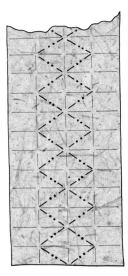

**8** Now make careful diagonal *mountain* folds across the middle, as shown, making sure your folds exactly connect at the intersections of existing creases. It may help to draw the line of the new folds with a pencil before creasing. This is a tricky step. Make sure the creases do not stray towards the outer edges of the sheet, and make them firm.

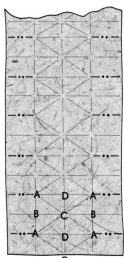

**9** Along the two outer edge sections, re-crease alternate valley creases to make them mountains as shown. This will produce a pleated effect along the edges, with diamonds across the middle. Locate As, Bs, Cs, and Ds.

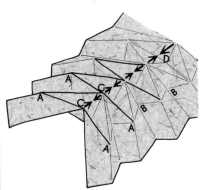

**10** Now squeeze the pleats together on both edges so that the side and end points (C and A) of the diamond rise up, and the middle point (D) of the diamond and pleat (B) cave in.

**11** Compress the pleats all along the strip, concertina fashion. Press firmly to reinforce all the creases, and then turn over.

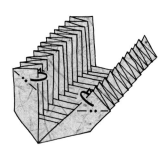

**12** Mountain fold the single layer corners inside at both front ends.

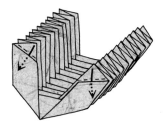

**13** Valley fold the double layer corners on the inside edges, as shown. Repeat all the way down the row of pleats, neatly folding in each corner in turn.

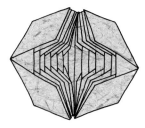

**14** Bring the ends round and together to form the bauble shape.

**15** Tuck the left-hand edge under the right, as shown, locking the bauble.

**16** The Bauble complete. To hang it, simply use a needle and thread to fix a loop to the top of the bauble. Alternatively, before locking the ends of the bauble together (see Step 15), attach a blob of plasticine to the free ends of a loop of thread and position it inside the body of the bauble, allowing the loop to issue from the top. The locking action will enclose the plasticine and hold the thread firmly in place.

# ANGEL

*DESIGNED BY DAVE BRILL, UK*

This elegant, semi-abstract design is far removed from the literal style of representation seen in some models. It succeeds well in capturing the likeness of a subject with just a few folds – just as difficult as using many. The Angel can be used to decorate the front of a Christmas card, or attached to the top of the Christmas tree with a loop of sticky tape.

**STAR RATING ★★**

**PAPERS**

A rectangle of mediumweight paper or foil, proportioned 3:2, or a sheet of A4 or A5 paper are all suitable for this piece.

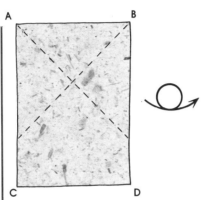

**1** Fold A over to the right so that it lies on edge BD. Crease and unfold. Repeat, folding B over to the left to lie on edge AC. Crease, unfold, and turn over.

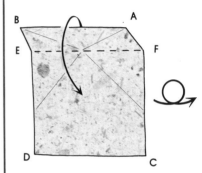

**3** Make a horizontal valley fold which passes through the centrepoint of the mountain 'cross'. Turn back over.

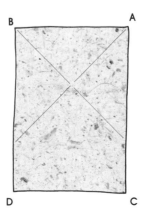

**2** The creases now rise towards you.

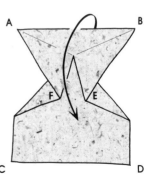

**4** Holding the sides of the paper at E and F, let A and B rise up as the sides are brought inwards . . .

27

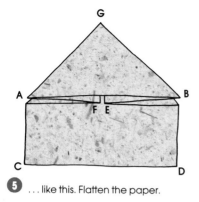

**5** . . . like this. Flatten the paper.

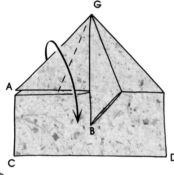

**6** Imagine a centre crease from the top point (G) down the middle of the paper. Fold in A and B to lie along that imaginary crease. Keep it neat at G. B has already been folded.

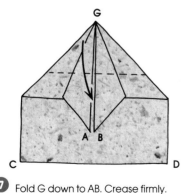

**7** Fold G down to AB. Crease firmly.

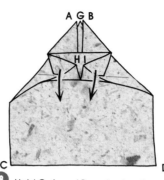

**8** Hold G, A and B and swing them back up to where G used to be at the top. Keep a firm hold of them. The paper does not lie flat in the middle.

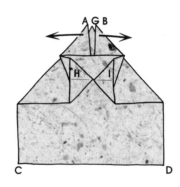

**9** Flatten the paper to form triangles H and I. Hold the paper with your left hand at H, and . . .

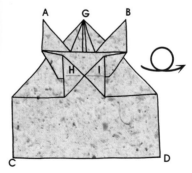

**10** . . . pull B and A away from G (see the next drawing to check the new position). Flatten and crease. Turn over.

**11** Fold in the sides so that they overlap in the centre (see next drawing). Note that they do not quite meet at G. C has already been folded.

**12** Tuck D and C behind. Fold down G. Carefully pleat the wings.

**13** The Angel complete.

# STREAMER

*DESIGNED BY ED SULLIVAN, USA*

**H**ere is a model which can be as long as you like! Learn the technique on one strip, fold another, and then join them together by glueing the last pleat of one to the first pleat of another. Repeat as many times as you wish, being careful to fold all sections from identical strips. The result is spectacular.

**1** With the right side of the paper facing you, mountain fold edge AB on a diagonal, so that AB lies under the bottom edge of the strip.

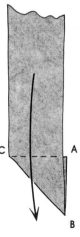

**2** Fold the length of the strip down along horizontal crease CA.

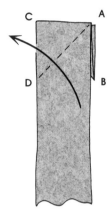

**3** Now fold the strip to the left along diagonal crease DA. Be careful to keep all the layers lined up at the edges.

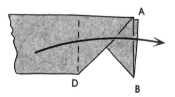

**4** Fold the strip to the right, making a vertical crease.

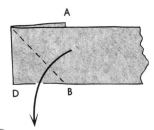

**5** Fold the strip down along a diagonal crease. Keep the layers lined up.

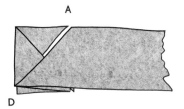

**8** Continue the sequence established above until the whole strip is folded up. Be extremely careful to keep all the layers lined up exactly.

**11** Fold valley creases through the exact point where the diagonals intersect. Note that both diagonals are mountain creases, and all horizontals are valleys.

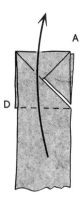

**6** Fold the strip back up making a horizontal crease . . .

**9** Unfold the strip to see this crease pattern along the strip.

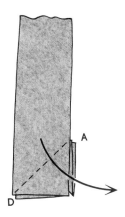

**7** . . . and then fold to the right along a diagonal crease.

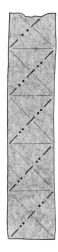

**10** Now mountain fold the other diagonals on each square, all along the strip. Keep it neat, and be careful to make the creases the same way up as the existing diagonals.

**12** The creases made in Step 11 form squares along the strip. Mountain fold diagonals on these squares just formed, connecting the top left- to the bottom right-hand corners of each square . . .

31

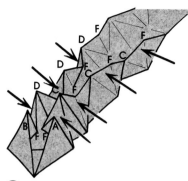

**13** ... and then the top right to the bottom left corners. Keep it neat!

**14** Make valley folds midway between the existing valley creases. These new creases each pass through two mountain diagonal 'crosses'. This is the completed crease pattern. Check that when you look at the paper all the diagonal creases are mountains, all the horizontals are valleys, and all the creases join, connect or intersect with accuracy. Identify AB, Cs, Ds, Es and Fs. Turn over

**15** Hold the edges of the strip at the first DC pair along from BA. Push them together gently and E should collapse downwards. Push a few more DC pairs together moving along the strip. F should tuck in and down on top. Continue like this, pushing BA up, to concertina up all the Es and to reinforce the creases. Note that all creases form – nothing is wasted.

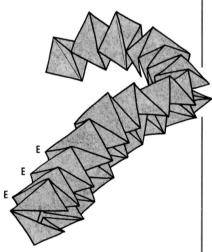

**16** When concertinaed, the strip will look something like this. Repeat with as many strips of identical width as you wish to fold. Glue them into one enormously long strip. Alternatively, bend one end of the streamer round to meet the other and glue to form a circular decoration. If the creases need to be redefined, push the ends towards each other, squeezing the concertina flat together. The streamer can be stored easily in this position from one Christmas to the next.

# BELL

### DESIGNED BY PAUL JACKSON, UK

Inflatable origami – blow-ups – are always fun to make, but there are very few such models; the Waterbomb is perhaps the best known.

When folding, leave a small hole at the bottom corner to blow into. Do not close it completely by folding *too* neatly! If the hole *is* too small, snip it open with scissors.

**STAR RATING ★★★**

**PAPERS**
Use a 15–20 cm (6–8 in) square of light- or mediumweight paper or foil.

**OTHER EQUIPMENT**
To suspend the bell you will need a needle and thread.

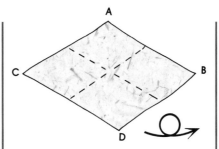

**1** Fold horizontal and vertical valley folds across the paper. Turn over, so that the creases rise towards you.

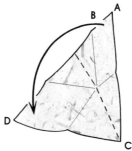

**2** Fold A over to D as shown. Unfold. Repeat this move, folding B over to C.

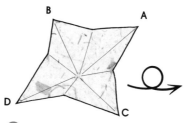

**3** The crease pattern should look like this. The paper is three-dimensional. Turn over so that the middle rises up. Push the horizontal and vertical mountain folds towards each other so that the central peak rises up, as shown. Four triangles are formed, meeting at E.

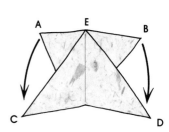

**4** Flatten the paper so that two triangles lie either side of the centre.

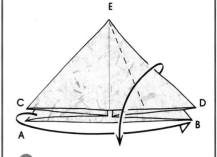

**5** Fold D inwards so that edge ED lies along the centre crease. (It may help to mark ABCD in pencil.) Swing A on the left around the back to the right so that it lies behind B.

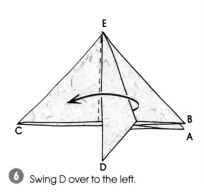

**6** Swing D over to the left.

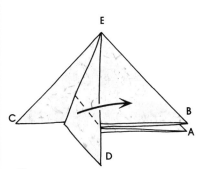

**7** Fold up D as shown so that it lies along edge CB.

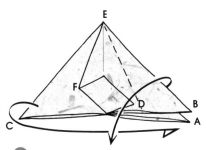

**8** The paper now looks like this. The folds in Steps 5–7 are now repeated with B, then A and then C. As in Step 5, fold B inwards so that edge EB lies along the centre crease, covering D. Swing C on the left around the back to lie behind A on the right.

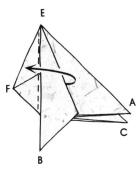

**9** Swing B over to the left to lie on top of F. Fold up B like D in Step 7.

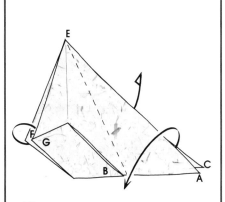

**10** As in Step 5, fold A inwards so that edge EA lies along the centre crease, covering B. Swing F on the left around the back to lie hidden behind C on the right. Swing A over to the left to lie on top of G. Fold up A like D in Step 7.

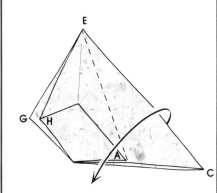

**11** As in Step 5, fold C inwards so that edge EC lies along the centre crease, covering A.

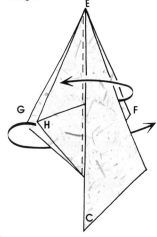

**12** Swing G on the left around the back and to the right to lie behind F. Swing C over to the left, to lie on top of H.

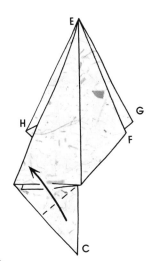

**13** Fold up corner C, as shown. Crease flat.

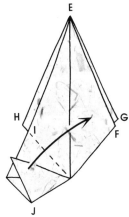

**14** Fold the flap up as shown . . .

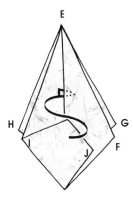

**15** . . . and slide J under the edge that runs down the centre of the paper, pushing it deep into the pocket.

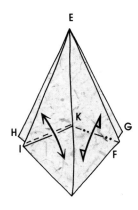

**16** The paper is now symmetrical. Carefully form valley creases between I and K, and H and K on the left and mountain creases between F and K, and G and K on the right. Do not crease beyond the centre.

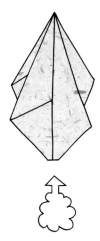

**18** At the bottom end, there should be a small hole. Blow into it and the bell should inflate! Inflating it is easier if the four flaps are spread apart and if the hole is clearly visible. The flexible creases just made will form a definite rim to the bell.

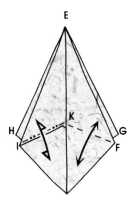

**17** Now make mountain creases on the left and valleys on the right, placing these creases on top of the previous ones. This will form creases that can bend backwards and forwards. Bend them to and fro several times so that they are very flexible.

**19** The Bell complete. To suspend, attach a loop to the top of the bell with needle and thread.

# STAR

*DESIGNED BY PAUL JACKSON, UK*

**A** good way to form geometric shapes is to fold a number of simple shapes which can interlock. This is commonly known as 'modular origami'. The Star is a simple example of this kind of folding, and to experiment try folding six, eight or more modules to make stars with more than four points.

---

**STAR RATING ★★**

**PAPERS**
You will need four sheets of lightweight paper or foil about 10 cm (4 in ) square in two colours or textures which work well together. Choosing complementary papers with care always adds to the finished piece.

**OTHER EQUIPMENT**
To suspend the star you will need a needle and thread.

---

**1** Fold B over to D. Crease and unfold.

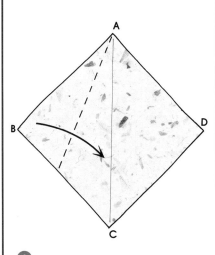

**2** Fold in edge AB to lie along crease AC.

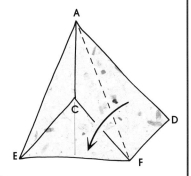

**3** Fold up C along a crease which follows edge EB, covering B.

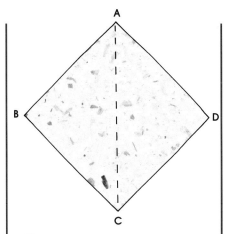

**4** Fold in edge AD to the centre so that it half covers C.

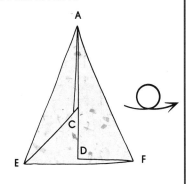

**5** The paper looks like this. Turn over.

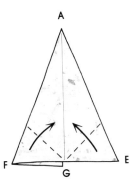

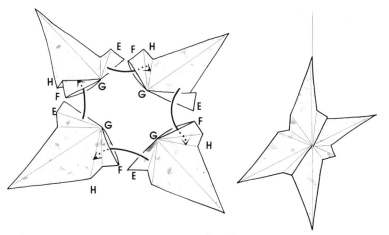

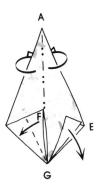

**6** Fold in F and E to lie along crease AG.

**7** Fold F and E back out to the sloping edges just formed which meet at G. E is shown already folded. Keep the folds neat at G.

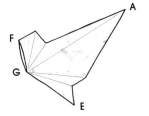

**8** Unfold the last two steps so it looks like this. This is one point of the star. Make three more sections just the same as the first, but make two of them in another (maybe patterned) paper.

**9** Tuck corner E of one section in between the layers of another at F and continue to push it further in until E touches H and the two Gs touch. The mountain and valley creases should line up where they overlap. In the same way, tuck in the third and fourth sections, alternating the types of paper, and finally locking the first section into the fourth. Strengthen and sharpen all the creases.

**10** The Star complete. To suspend, attach a loop to one point of the star with needle and thread.

**2**

# CHILDREN'S
# PARTIES

★ ★ ★ ★ ★

# BOW TIE

▬

*DESIGNED BY PAUL JACKSON, UK*

**S**imple to make and fun to wear, the Bow Tie is an ideal way of breaking the ice at parties for all age groups!

Decorate the Bow Tie with some self-adhesive coloured shapes – dots or squares, for example – for a truly individual effect.

---

**STAR RATING ★**

**PAPERS**

Use a good quality 4-ply paper napkin, or fold two 2-ply napkins together. A single 2-ply napkin will make a floppy bow tie.

**OTHER EQUIPMENT**

Elastic band, approximate diameter 3½ cm (1½ in); cord elastic, 30 cm (12 in) in length. To decorate the bow tie use self-adhesive coloured shapes.

---

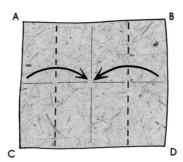

**1** Fold the napkin in half horizontally and vertically. Unfold. Fold AC and BD to the central vertical crease.

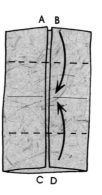

**2** Fold AB and CD to the central horizontal crease.

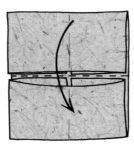

**3** Fold in half across the middle.

**4** The folding is now complete.

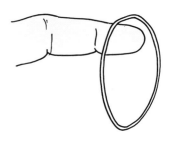

**5** Take the elastic band . . .

**6** . . . and wrap it around a finger three times.

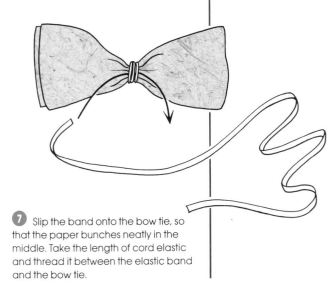

**7** Slip the band onto the bow tie, so that the paper bunches neatly in the middle. Take the length of cord elastic and thread it between the elastic band and the bow tie.

**8** Tie the ends of the cord elastic together, decorate the front of the bow with self-adhesive coloured shapes, if wished, and the Bow Tie is ready to wear.

# BUFFET SERVER

*TRADITIONAL*

**T**his is a practical and quick-to-make design that is ideal for buffets – to pre-wrap sets of cutlery – or for children's parties.

**STAR RATING ★**

**PAPERS**

Use paper napkins; 4-ply is the best, but 3- or 2-ply are adequate. Starched linen napkins may also be used.

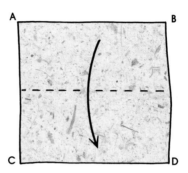

**1** If the napkin is already folded into quarters (as most are), skip forward to Step 3. Otherwise, fold AB down to CD.

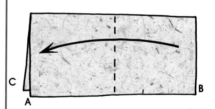

**2** Then fold BD across to AC.

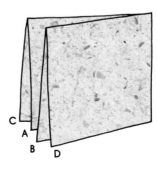

**3** Note CABD. Rotate to the Step 4 position.

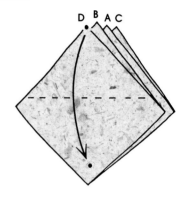

**4** Fold down D almost to the bottom corner.

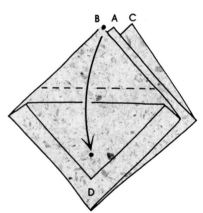

**5** Fold B almost to D.

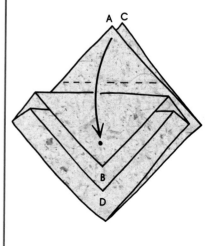

**6** Fold A almost to B

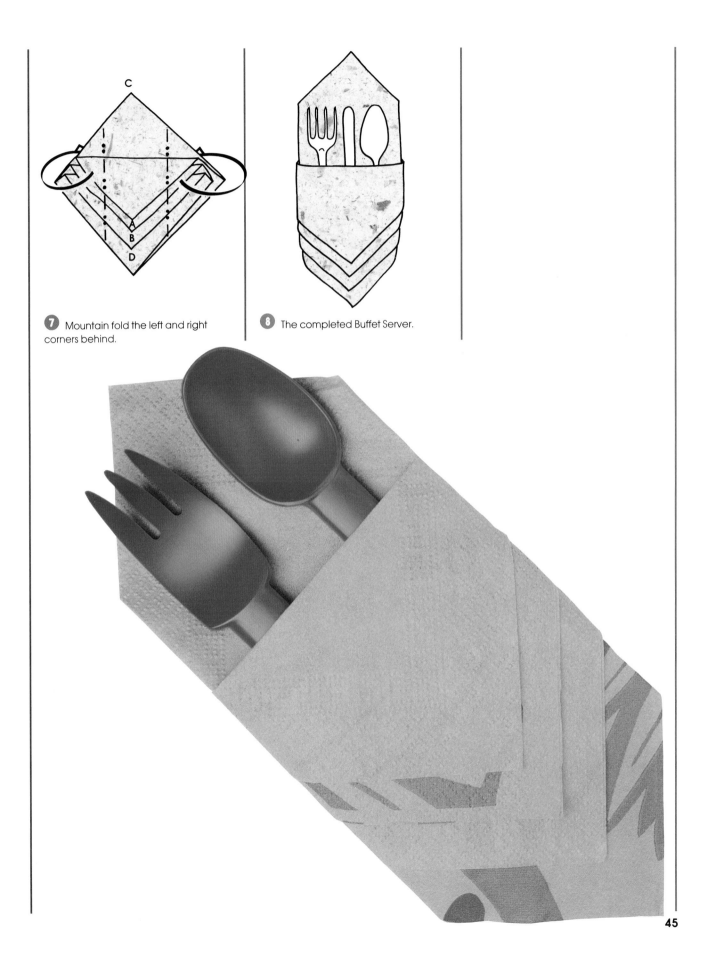

**7** Mountain fold the left and right corners behind.

**8** The completed Buffet Server.

# TOOT-FLUTE

## *TRADITIONAL*

**O**f the few musical instruments that can be made from paper, this is perhaps the simplest and you will be amazed by the sound it produces. A must for any children's party, get your young guests to make their own and mount a competition for the loudest 'toot'!

**STAR RATING ★**

**PAPERS**

Use a lightweight sheet of A4 paper. For deeper musical tones, use larger sheets; for higher tones, use smaller ones. The Toot-Flute can also be made from a paper drinking straw, cut to a point at one end rather like the nib of a fountain pen, and then snipped in the appropriate place to give it an arrowhead shape.

**OTHER EQUIPMENT**

Pencil; sticky tape; scissors (safety scissors if children are making their own toot-flutes).

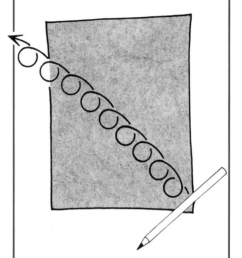

**1** Wrap a corner of the paper around a pencil and roll it across the sheet at 45° to the edge.

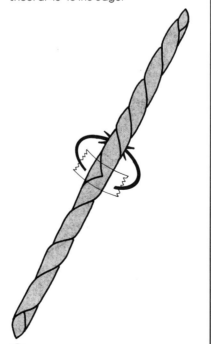

**2** Drop the pencil out and secure the loose corner with a piece of sticky tape.

**3** Starting from the notch at one end, make a cut to free A . . .

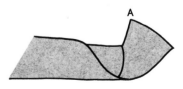

**4** . . . like this.

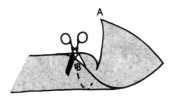

**5** Repeat at the other side of the notch, to free B.

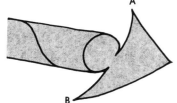

**6** Note that the triangle is joined to the tube by only a small edge. The smaller the edge, the easier the triangle will vibrate and so the louder the flute will sound.

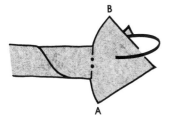

**7** Fold the triangle against the tube.

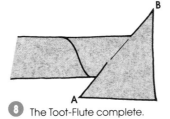

**8** The Toot-Flute complete.

**BELOW** With the triangle at the bottom of the flute, *suck* gently and the flute will buzz! Alternatively, put the triangle into your mouth (be careful not to wet it) and *blow* gently to produce a buzz too.

# PIRATE'S HAT
# AND SHIRT

*TRADITIONAL*

**M**any readers will be familiar with the basic triangular hat shown in Step 5, but few will know that it can be developed into the stronger Pirate's Hat at Step 10 and later torn to create the fun Shirt. Step 13 could even be a pirate ship!

Provide a Step 10 pirate hat for each child (or adult, if it's that sort of party!), and then choose an appropriate moment to show how the hat can become a shirt. Stand back, and watch the chaos as everyone makes their own!

**STAR RATING ★★**

**PAPERS**
Use a complete double-page leaf from a broadsheet (large format) newspaper.

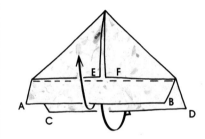

**1** Fold in half from top to bottom.

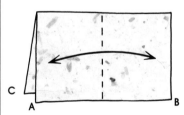

**4** Fold up edge AB along a crease which runs along the bottom of triangles E and F and, similarly, fold up CD behind.

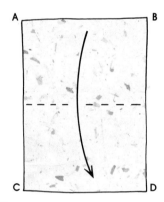

**2** Fold in half, left to right. Unfold.

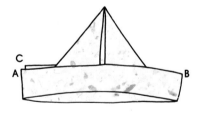

**5** This makes a simple, though rather large and floppy, hat.

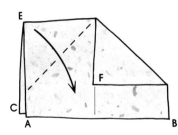

**3** Fold corners E and F to the centre crease. F is shown already folded.

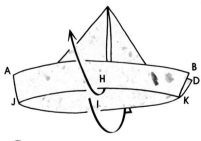

**6** Hold as shown at H and I. Pull H and I apart, so that J and K come towards each other.

**OPPOSITE** To complete the Pirate's Hat and Shirt, turn the page for the remaining instructions.

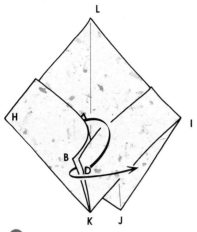

**7** This makes a diamond shape. Tuck D behind B to flatten the front. Repeat behind, tucking A under C.

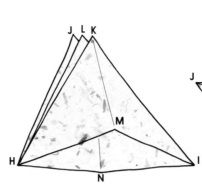

**10** As you did in Step 6, open up the bottom to form the Pirate's Hat. To make the Pirate's Shirt, bring H and I together by pulling M and N apart, as in Steps 6–7.

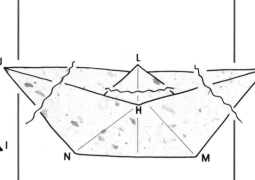

**13** Could this be a pirate ship? Tear off J, K and L as shown. Carefully, completely unfold the remainder of the ship.

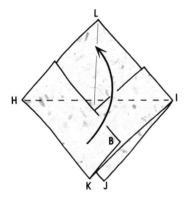

**8** Fold K up to L, and behind fold J to L.

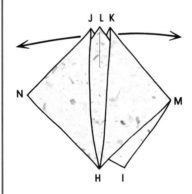

**11** Hold K and J and pull them away from L . . .

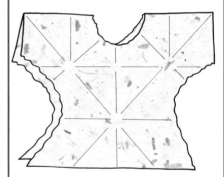

**14** And here is the Pirate's Shirt!

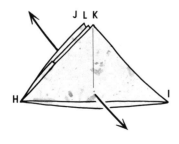

**9** It should look like this.

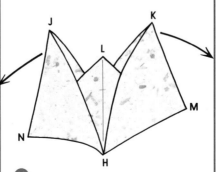

**12** . . . like this. Continue to pull until Step 13 is made.

# SUN HAT

## *DESIGNED BY PAUL JACKSON, UK*

**N**o party is complete without a party hat, but on this model the visor gives good protection from the sun, so it can be worn both in and out of doors.

**STAR RATING ★★**

**PAPERS**

Use a sheet of mediumweight paper, proportioned 5:8. For a child's head, use a sheet 25 x 40 cm (10 x 16 in).

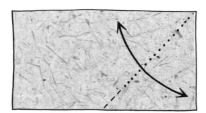

**1** Bring the bottom right-hand corner up to the top edge, in such a way that if a crease was made it would start at the top right corner. However, do not make a crease, but instead make a short pinch at the bottom edge.

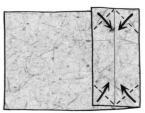

**4** Turn in the corners to the centre crease in the flap.

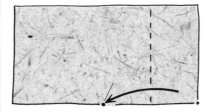

**2** Fold the bottom corner to the pinch.

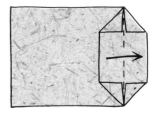

**5** Fold the flap in half, left to right, creating a pocket.

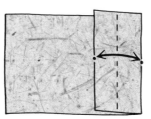

**3** Fold the flap in half. Unfold.

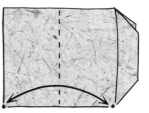

**6** Fold the bottom left corner to the edge of the pocket. Unfold.

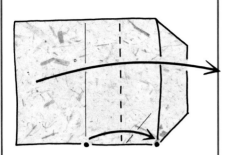

**7** Fold the Step 6 crease to the edge of the pocket.

**8** Turn in the corners to the Step 6 crease.

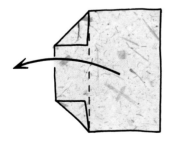

**9** Fold the loose flap back to the left.

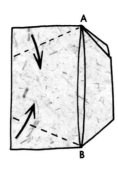

**10** Turn in the corners a little. Note the gash between A and B.

**11** Fold the loose flap across to the right.

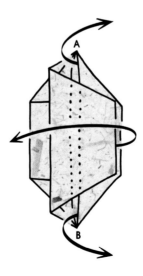

**12** Lift up the top flap and open out the gash between A and B, creating a box form . . .

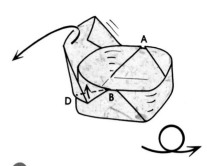

**13** . . . like this. Swivel the visor out and to the left, and crease DB (repeat at back) to hold the visor in place. If the angle of the visor is too high or too low, re-crease Step 11 in another position. Turn over.

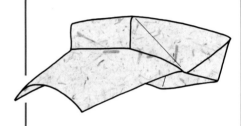

**14** The Sun Hat complete.

# DOGGY BAG

*DESIGNED BY PAUL JACKSON, UK*

**H**ere is a cheap and fun way to make a sturdy bag for your party guests to take away their gifts and goodies.

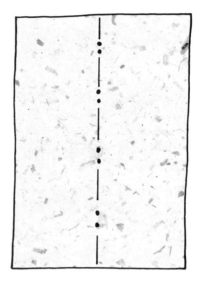

**1** Make a mountain fold down the middle. Unfold.

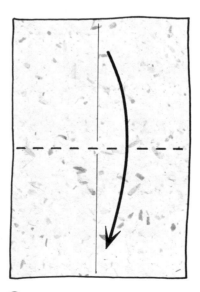

**2** Fold the top edge down to the bottom.

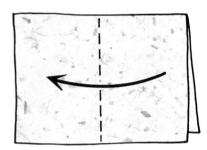

**3** Fold the right edge across to the left.

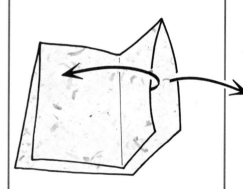

**4** Let the right-hand side stand upright. Pull open the layers . . .

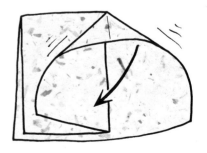

**5** . . . and squash flat . . .

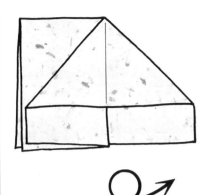

**6** . . . like this. Turn over.

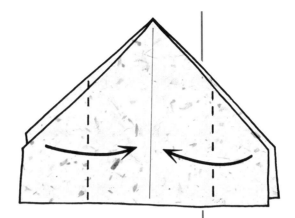

**9** Fold the sides to the middle. Repeat behind.

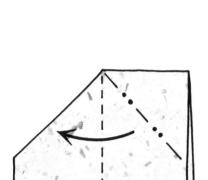

**7** Repeat steps 3–6 on this side.

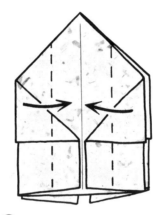

**10** Again, fold the sides to the middle. Repeat behind.

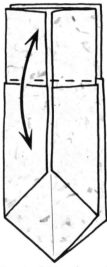

**12** Fold and unfold as shown. Repeat behind.

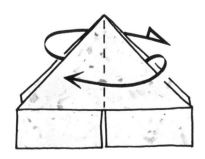

**8** Swivel the front edge at the right across to the left, and swivel the rear edge at the left across to the right.

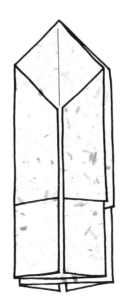

**11** Turn the paper upside-down.

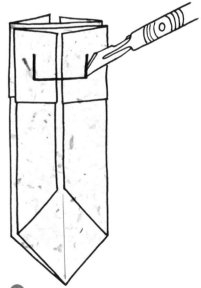

**13** With a craft knife, using a metal ruler as a guide, cut through all the layers as shown.

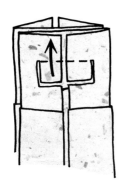

**14** Fold up all the layers as shown . . .

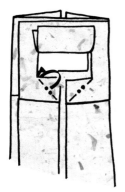

**15** . . . to create a handle for the bag. Tuck in the loose corners. Repeat behind.

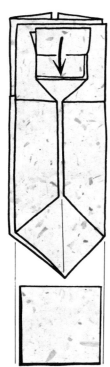

**16** Unfold the handle. For added strength, cut out a square of card a little smaller than the width of the bag.

**17** Push up the bottom to open the bag.

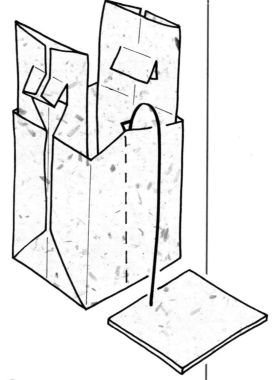

**18** Put the card into the bag and close up the handles.

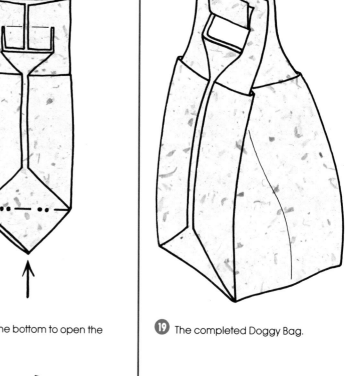

**19** The completed Doggy Bag.

# 3

# FESTIVE MEALS

★ ★ ★ ★ ★

# COCKADE NAPKIN

*TRADITIONAL*

**T**his is one of the most decorative and spectacular napkin folds, impressive enough to use on the most important occasions.

**STAR RATING ★★**

**PAPERS**

Use a 4-ply paper napkin for the best results, although 3- and 2-ply are adequate.

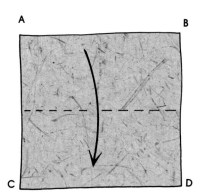

**1** If the napkin is already folded into quarters (as most are), skip forward to Step 3; otherwise, fold AB down to CD.

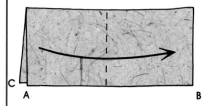

**2** Fold AC across to BD.

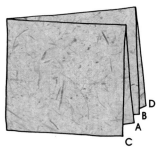

**3** Note CABD. Rotate to Step 4 position.

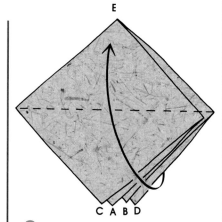

**4** Fold CABD up to E.

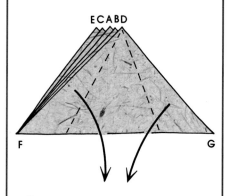

**5** Fold the sloping edges of the triangle inwards so that FE and GE meet in the middle.

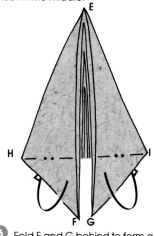

**6** Fold F and G behind to form a straight edge between H and I.

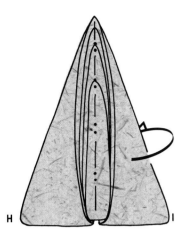

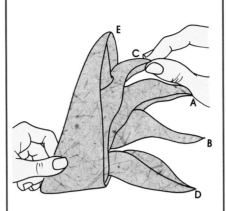

**7** Fold I behind, folding the shape in half down the middle.

**8** Grip H and I firmly with one hand. With the other hand pull D out as far as possible from the nest of layers. Repeat with B (not pulling it as far as D) and likewise pull out A, and finally C.

**9** The Cockade Napkin complete.

# PLACE CARD

### DESIGNED BY PAUL JACKSON, UK

**A** finishing touch to a place setting is to make a card which carries the name of the guest who is to sit there. This same design can also hold photographs, artwork, or give exhibition information.

---

**STAR RATING ★**

**PAPERS**
Use a mediumweight paper of A4 size for the frame, and thin card for the insert.

**OTHER EQUIPMENT**
Scissors or craft knife and metal ruler; writing pen.

---

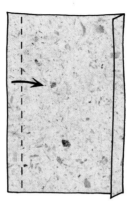

**1** Fold in about 1 cm (½ in) along the longer edges. The right-hand side is shown already folded.

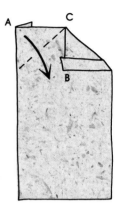

**3** Fold A and B into the middle, using the pinch at C to find the point on the top edge where the creases meet. B is shown already folded.

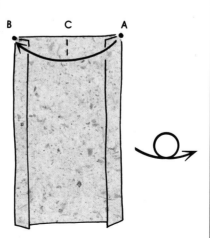

**2** Bring top corners A and B together and pinch to locate the middle of the top edge (C). Do not make a long crease. Unfold and turn over.

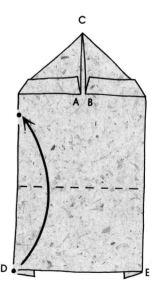

**4** Fold up D and E to lie just below the base of the triangle. The exact placement is unimportant.

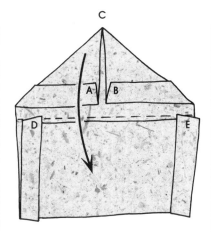

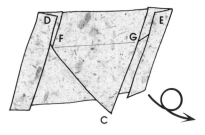

**5** Fold down C and crease along a line just above DE.

**7** This is the back of the place-card holder, with C forming a stand. Turn over.

**9** The Place Card complete.

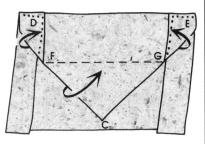

**6** Flip loose corners D and E to the front, trapping the corners of the large C triangle behind them. Make a valley crease between F and G, lifting corner C.

**8** Measure the proportions of the holder. Cut a piece of paper or card which is fractionally smaller. Write the person's name on it and tuck the short edges into the pockets at the sides of the place-card holder.

# NAPKIN RING

*DESIGNED BY PAUL JACKSON, UK*

**I**nstead of folding paper napkins, roll up linen napkins and present them at the side of each place setting inside the napkin ring described here. The effect is less flamboyant, but just as impressive.

To personalize each napkin ring, stencil a monogram, initial or image, such as a flower, onto the central shield.

**STAR RATING ★★★**

**PAPERS**
Use a 2:1 rectangle of light- or mediumweight paper, approximately 20 x 10 cm (8 x 4 in).

**OTHER EQUIPMENT**
To decorate the napkin ring you will need a purchased or homemade stencil; brush and paints, or colouring pencils, felt tip pens, etc.

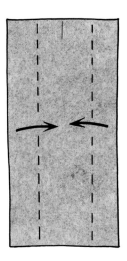

**1** As you did in Step 2 of the Place Card, fold the top edge in half and pinch to locate the centre of the edge. Then fold the long edges into the middle, using the pinch as a location point.

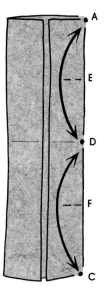

**3** Fold A to D making only a short crease at the right-hand edge (E), and unfold. Repeat, folding C to D, to make F.

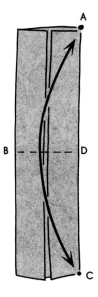

**2** Fold A down to C to make crease BD. Unfold.

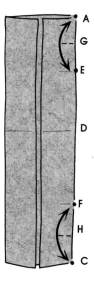

**4** Fold A to E, making a short crease at the right-hand edge (G). Repeat, folding C to F, to make H.

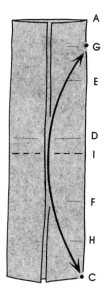

**5** Fold C up to G. Crease right across to make I and unfold.

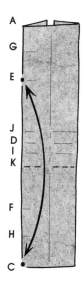

**7** This is the crease pattern at present. Fold C up to E. Crease right across to make K and unfold.

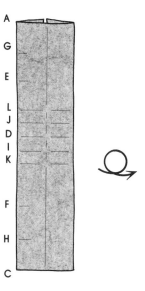

**9** This is now the crease pattern. Turn over.

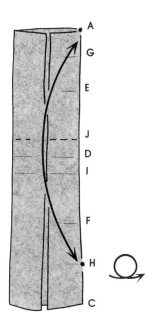

**6** Fold A down to H. Crease right across to make J and unfold. Turn over.

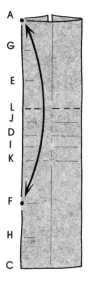

**8** Fold A down to F. Crease right across to make L and unfold.

**10** Fold the long edges into the middle. Unfold.

65

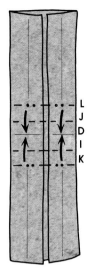

**11** Pleat along the existing creases, bringing K and L to D.

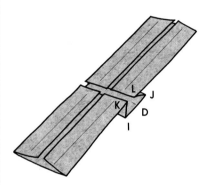

**12** It should now look like this.

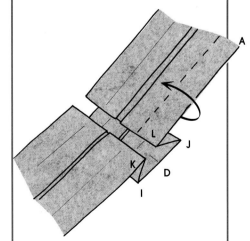

**13** Fold the long edge AL in towards the middle along the crease made in Step 10.

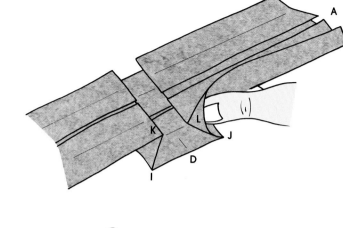

**14** Dig your thumb into the pocket between L and J, forming a curved arc. Squash it flat into a triangle . . .

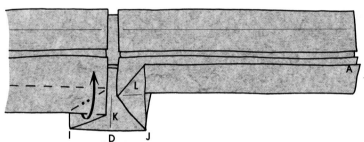

**15** . . . like this. Repeat with K, folding it across, pulling it into an arc, digging a thumb in the pocket under K, and squashing it to make a triangle. The points of the triangles should meet.

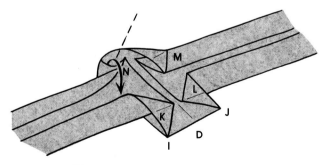

**16** Now fold in the long edges on the opposite side of the strip, but instead of digging your thumb in the pockets as you did under K and L, swing M and N right across, opening up another pocket. Squash this flat forming a triangle. The points of the triangles point away from each other, the long sides meeting.

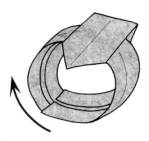

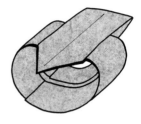

**18** Feed one end of the strap into the other to fasten the ring.

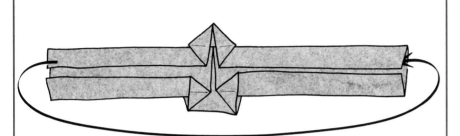

**17** It should look like this. When turned over there should be a simple shield shape on the reverse.

**19** The Napkin Ring complete.

# CORNUCOPIA NAPKIN

*TRADITIONAL*

Ideal for Thanksgiving or Harvest Festival meals, this is a simple but elegant folded napkin. Use a piece of fruit to hold it open.

**STAR RATING ★**

**PAPERS**
Use 4-ply napkins for the best results.

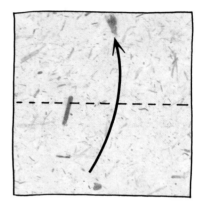

❶ Fold the bottom edge of an open napkin up to the top.

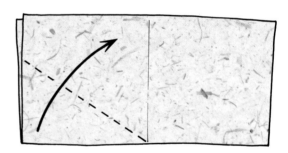

❷ Fold in the bottom left-hand corner, as shown.

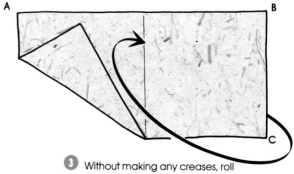

❸ Without making any creases, roll BC across to the left, so that C comes to rest against the middle of the top edge . . .

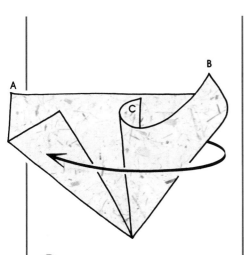

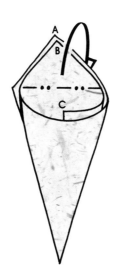

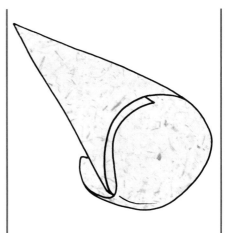

**4** . . . like this. Continue to roll, so that B comes to rest in front of A.

**5** To lock, fold A and B behind.

**6** The Cornucopia Napkin complete.

# FLORAL CENTREPIECE

*IRIS: TRADITIONAL JAPANESE*
*LEAVES AND VASE:*
*DESIGNED BY PAUL JACKSON, UK*

**O**f all the projects in the book, this is the one that will require the most time, the most equipment and will take the most artistry to design and arrange. That said, it is also the project that will be the most admired. It makes a stunning centrepiece to any room or dining table for any occasion. Choose your papers with great care, co-ordinating the colours, tones and textures.

## STAR RATING ★★★★

### PAPERS

For the **iris**, use light- or mediumweight paper approximately 15–20 cm (6–8 in) square.

For the **leaves**, use mediumweight paper 20–25 cm (8–10 in) square – the paper should be a little larger than that used for the iris.

For the **vase**, use heavyweight paper 25–35 cm (10–14 in) square – the paper should be 1½ times the size of that used for the iris. For a particularly sturdy vase, use thick artist's paper – Ingres or watercolour paper – and employ the 'wet folding' process explained in the section on Papers (see Introduction).

### OTHER EQUIPMENT

Pencil; scissors; florist's wires (3 or 4 for each stem); gutta tape (green binding tape, available from florist's shops); sticky tape; glue; and tapioca balls or rice grains.

## IRIS

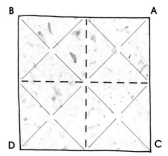

**1** Crease the two diagonals, both valleys. Turn over.

**3** Valley fold in half vertically and unfold. Valley fold in half horizontally.

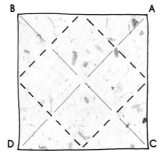

**2** The creases now rise towards you. Fold the four corners into the middle. Unfold.

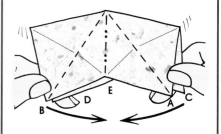

**4** Push the four corners together into the middle so that the valley folds on the diagonals collapse inwards . . .

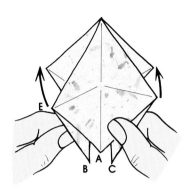

**5** . . . and four triangular flaps are formed in a star shape. Flatten the paper so that there are two flaps either side of the centre . . .

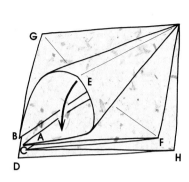

**8** Continue to press on E, until it squashes flat. Crease it firmly.

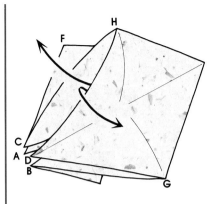

**11** . . . and press down on the fold to open its pocket, as in Step 8, to squash H flat. Keep the points ABCD together.

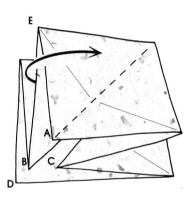

**6** . . . like this. Lift E so that it stands vertically.

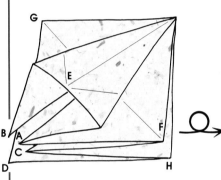

**9** Turn over.

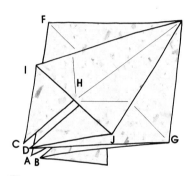

**12** It should now look like this. Fold I over to touch J. Then lift F so that it stands upright. Press down on the fold to squash it flat. Turn over and repeat with G.

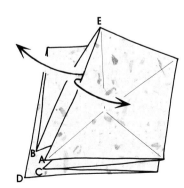

**7** Press the folded edge to open the pocket inside E. Hold ABCD neatly together.

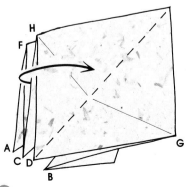

**10** Lift up H . . .

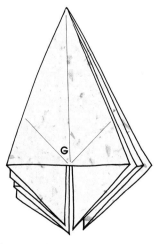

**13** All four flaps are now squashed and the paper is symmetrical.

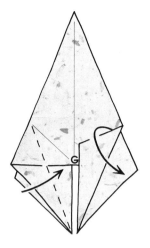

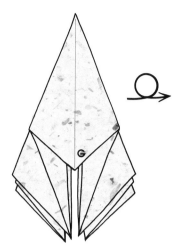

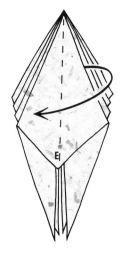

**14** Fold in the side points of the top layer at the lower, broader end to lie along the central crease, covering G. The right-hand side is shown already folded. Unfold.

**16** Turn over.

**18** The paper is now completely symmetrical with four layers on each side. Fold one layer from the right over to the left.

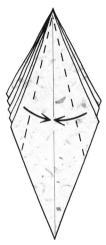

**19** This will expose a blank face. Fold in the top edges of the upper layer so they lie along the middle. Keep it neat!

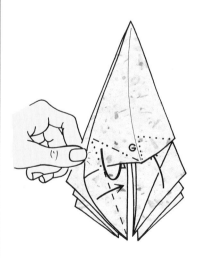

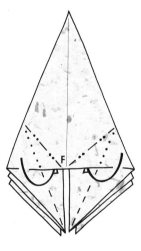

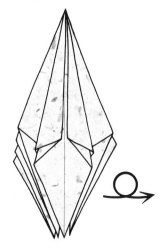

**15** With one hand, lift up G. With the other, re-form the creases made in the last step. Push these folds under G, using the old mountain creases made in Step 2, until the paper lies flat, as shown on the right of the diagram.

**17** Repeat Steps 14–16 on either side of F. There should now be four layers either side of the centre. Fold two layers on the right over to the left and turn over, so there are two layers on the left and six on the right. Fold two on the right over to the left . . . so that there are four layers on either side with H on top. Repeat Steps 14–16 with H. Turn over and repeat with E.

**20** This is the result. Turn over.

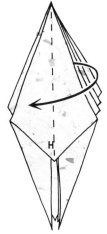

**21** Fold one layer over from right to left .

**22** Fold as in Step 19. Repeat the process on the other two blank faces. The paper will crease easier and neater if the layers are symmetrical.

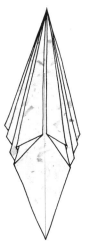

**23** It should now look like this. Move the layers around so that there are four either side of the centre, but so that the top layer is the one you have just folded. Turn upside down.

**24** The iris now has a narrow stem. Fold down the petal facing you . . .

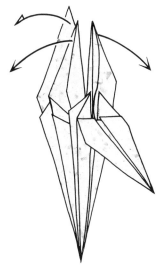

**25** . . . like this. Turn over, and fold down the petal. Repeat with the other two petals . . .

**26** . . . like this. Now loosely roll each of the petals in turn around a pencil. This will give them a soft, curled shape.

**27** The Iris complete.

73

## LEAVES AND STEM

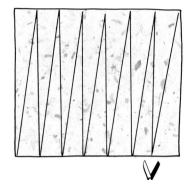

**1** Cut the square into long tapering strips, as shown. One square will make 12 or more leaves.

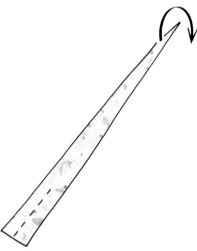

**2** Fold the paper in half at the square end by about 2½ cm (1 in). Curl the tip of the leaf.

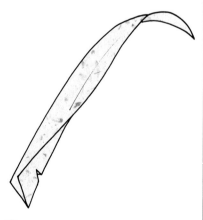

**3** With a pair of scissors, cut out a small V shape in the middle of the crease, not too near the end.

## WIRING UP

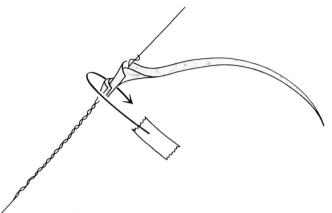

**1** Overlap two florist's wires and twist together. Overlap another wire and join it by twisting. For longer stems, simply twist in more wires. Poke one end of the wire through the cut in the leaf, position the leaf a little way down the wire, and then twist the square end of the leaf tight around the wire, at such an angle that the leaf points upwards, not horizontally. Secure the end of the twisted leaf with a piece of sticky tape.

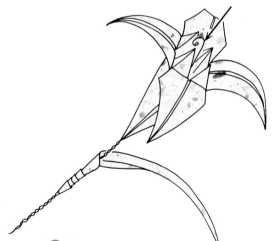

**2** Now push the end of the wire through the bottom of the iris. This can be tricky, but rather than cut the paper to make a hole, moisten it with your tongue. This should weaken the paper enough to push the wire through. Once through, bend over the top of the wire (as shown), and then drop the end of the wire back into the flower until it catches tight near the base of the stem. Wind green gutta tape onto the wire, starting at the bottom. At the top, carefully wind the tape round the base of the iris, pulling it very tight as you go to secure the iris to the wire. Wind the tape to the bottom of the stem.

# VASE

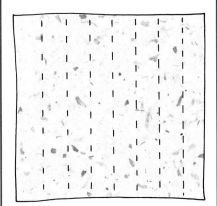

**1** Divide the square into eighths, making sure that all creases are valleys.

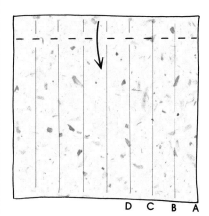

**2** Fold down the top edge by about 2½ cm (1 in). Turn over.

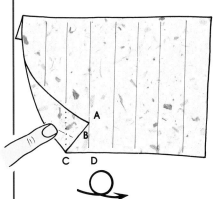

**3** Fold A across to touch the third crease (D) and make a sloping crease between the first and second creases (B and C) that will exactly touch C. Make sure this crease does not extend beyond the first and second creases.

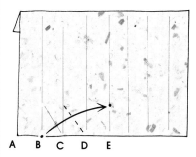

**4** Unfold, moving A back to its original position. The crease should be like this, to the left of C. Repeat Step 3, but this time folding B over to the fourth crease (E), and make a crease between C and D.

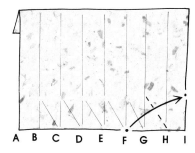

**5** Keep repeating this move by folding C to crease 5 (F), then D to crease 6 (G), E to crease 7 (H), and F to the right-hand edge (I). The creases should look like this.

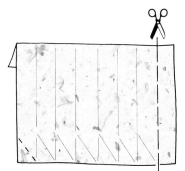

**6** Fold a crease which runs into B, from the left-hand edge, parallel to the crease which runs into C. Cut off the right-hand ⅛th of paper. Turn over.

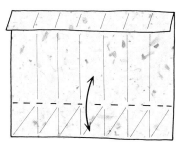

**7** Make a horizontal valley crease which connects the tops of all the sloping creases. Unfold.

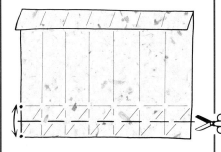

**8** Fold the bottom edge up to the horizontal crease just made. Then cut along this crease, discarding the bottom piece.

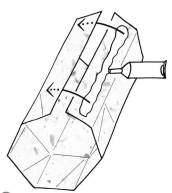

**9** Reinforce the vertical creases to form a tube. Glue the right-hand panel, then bring over the left-hand edge and tuck the right-hand panel under the flap at the top to help lock it in place. The vase now has six sides.

**10** Push the end of the vase in so the sloping creases all overlap each other, collapsing into the centre.

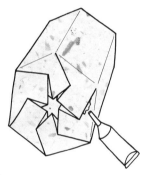

**11** Glue beneath the triangles to lock them in place.

**12** The completed Vase. Before arranging the flowers, weight the vase with tapioca balls or rice. This also helps the iris stems to stand straight, instead of falling to the vase's edge.

# 4

# EASTER

★ ★ ★ ★ ★

# EGG COSY

*DESIGNED BY PAUL JACKSON, UK*

**P**aper is an excellent insulator, so this design really will help to keep boiled eggs warm as well as adding a festive touch to the breakfast table.

**STAR RATING ★**

**PAPERS**
Use an oblong of lightweight paper about 20 x 15 cm (8 x 6 in).

**SPECIAL NOTE**
To begin this design complete Steps 1–7 of the Doggy Bag (see page 54) and then continue with the steps on this page.
Reverse folds are explained in detail in the section on Folding Techniques (see Introduction).

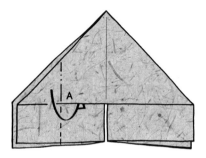

**1**  See Special Note. Reverse fold the front left layer into the middle. Note A. Repeat with the rear left layer.

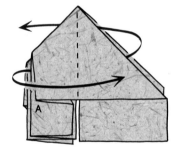

**2**  Swivel the front left layer across to the right and swivel the rear right layer across to the left.

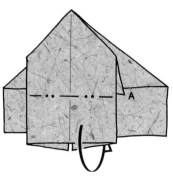

**3**  Fold the bottom edge into the pocket at A.

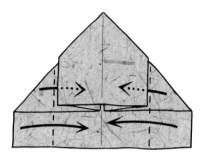

**4**  Tuck the sides into the middle.

**5**  Tuck the bottom edge into the pocket.

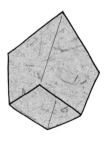

**6**  The completed Egg Cosy.

# CHICK

*DESIGNED BY PAUL JACKSON, UK*

**H**aving completed this design, you will see how, in origami terms, a chick could be said to be a blob with a beak. Once this is understood, it becomes an easy challenge for a paper folder to design a chick. Have a go yourself.

Make a clutch of chicks and some Easter Bunnies (see next project) to make a centrepiece for the dining table, or use one or two to decorate the top of an Easter cake.

**STAR RATING ★★**

**PAPERS**
You will need a lightweight yellow paper, 10 cm (4 in) square for each chick.

**OTHER EQUIPMENT**
Pencil.

**SPECIAL NOTE**
The reverse folds featured in Steps 10 and 11 are explained in detail in the section on Folding Techniques (see Introduction).

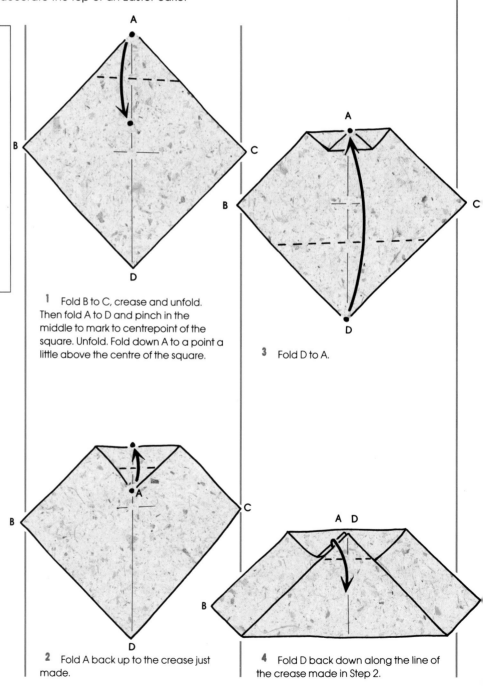

**1** Fold B to C, crease and unfold. Then fold A to D and pinch in the middle to mark to centrepoint of the square. Unfold. Fold down A to a point a little above the centre of the square.

**3** Fold D to A.

**2** Fold A back up to the crease just made.

**4** Fold D back down along the line of the crease made in Step 2.

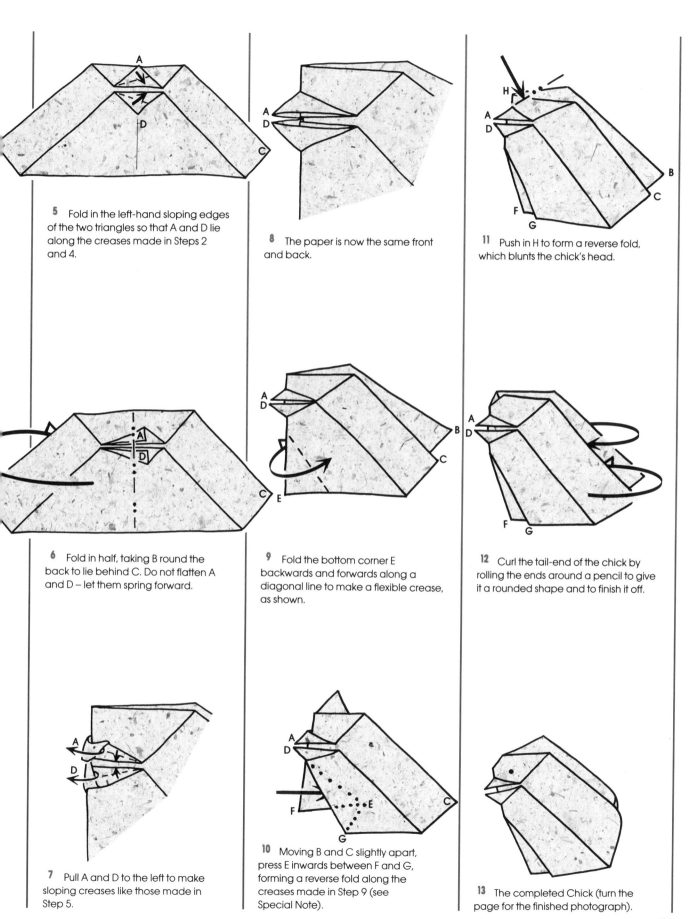

**5**  Fold in the left-hand sloping edges of the two triangles so that A and D lie along the creases made in Steps 2 and 4.

**8**  The paper is now the same front and back.

**11**  Push in H to form a reverse fold, which blunts the chick's head.

**6**  Fold in half, taking B round the back to lie behind C. Do not flatten A and D – let them spring forward.

**9**  Fold the bottom corner E backwards and forwards along a diagonal line to make a flexible crease, as shown.

**12**  Curl the tail-end of the chick by rolling the ends around a pencil to give it a rounded shape and to finish it off.

**7**  Pull A and D to the left to make sloping creases like those made in Step 5.

**10**  Moving B and C slightly apart, press E inwards between F and G, forming a reverse fold along the creases made in Step 9 (see Special Note).

**13**  The completed Chick (turn the page for the finished photograph).

# EASTER BUNNY

*DESIGNED BY AN UNKNOWN CREATOR
AND PAUL JACKSON*

**T**here are many origami bunnies, but here is one with a difference: it is one of the few made from two pieces, and the only one in which both sections are blow-ups.

**STAR RATING ★★**

**PAPERS**
Use two squares of lightweight paper, the head square about two-thirds the size of the body square, for each bunny.

**OTHER EQUIPMENT**
Paper glue.

**SPECIAL NOTE**
To begin both the Body and Head sections of this design, complete Steps 1–4 of the Bell (see page 34) and then continue with the instructions given here.

## BODY

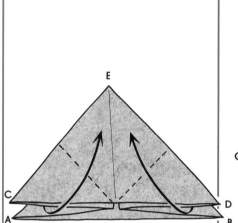

**1** See Special Note. Fold C and D up to E.

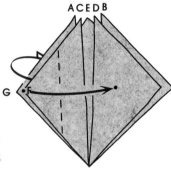

**3** Fold F across to the right so that it goes a little beyond the centre crease. Repeat behind with G.

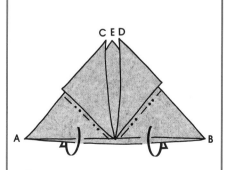

**2** Fold A and B behind to E.

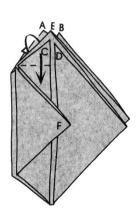

**4** Fold down corner C. Repeat behind with A.

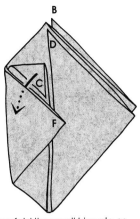

**5** Valley fold the small triangle as shown, and tuck it *between* the two layers of paper which run down to F. Repeat behind with A.

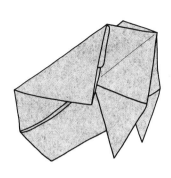

**8** The completed body.

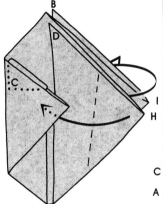

**6** Fold H across to the left, tucking it underneath F. Repeat behind with I.

## HEAD

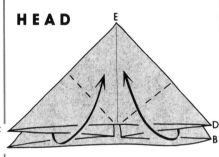

**1** See Special Note. Fold C and D up to E.

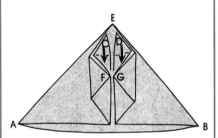

**3** Fold down C and D.

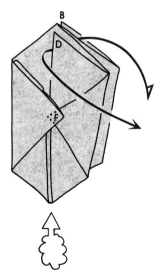

**7** Fold down D along the edge which runs down to H. Repeat with B behind. Carefully blow into the hole at the bottom to inflate the body (if necessary, you can enlarge the hole with the point of a pencil).

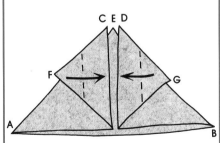

**2** Fold F and G into the middle.

**4** As in Step 5 of the body, valley fold the small triangles just formed where shown, and tuck them *between* the two layers of paper which run to F and G. Turn over.

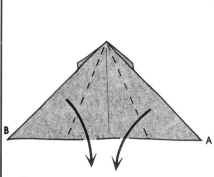

**5** Fold down B and A as shown.

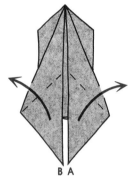

**6** Fold B and A back out at such an angle that BA forms a long horizontal edge. See Step 7 to check.

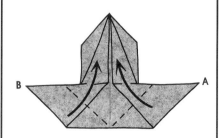

**7** Fold up B and A as shown, so that the bottom edge lies along the middle crease. These are the bunny's ears.

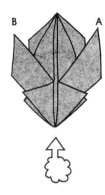

**8** It should look like this. As with the body, carefully blow into the hole at the bottom to inflate the head.

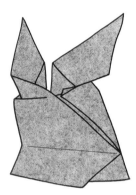

**9** The completed head. If needed, use a little paper glue to attach the head to the top of the body.

**10** The Easter Bunny fully assembled.

# EGG BASKET

*DESIGNED BY PAUL JACKSON, UK*

**T**his basket has clean lines and is very strongly locked together. It is ideal for displaying eggs at Eastertime, but can be used all year round as a presentation or storage bowl. Made with strong paper, it lasts a surprisingly long time.

**STAR RATING ★★**

**PAPERS**
Use heavyweight paper, 25–38 cm (10–15 in) square. For a very sturdy basket, use thick artist's paper – Ingres or watercolour paper – and employ the 'wet folding' process explained in the section on Papers (see Introduction).

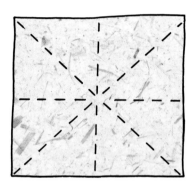

**1**  Crease as shown horizontally, vertically and diagonally, making sure that all creases are valleys.

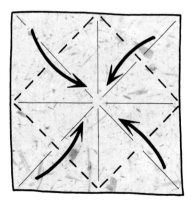

**2**  Fold the corners into the middle.

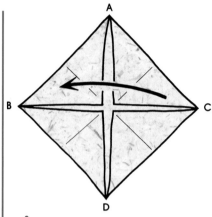

**3**  Fold C across to B.

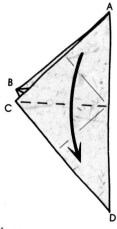

**4**  Fold A down to D.

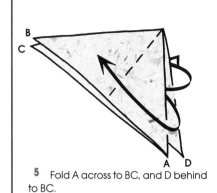

**5** Fold A across to BC, and D behind to BC.

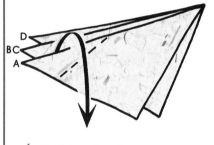

**6** Fold down A as shown.

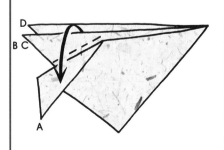

**7** Fold down BC on top of A.

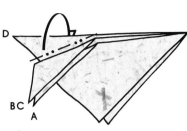

**8** Fold D behind. Unfold back to Step 3 position.

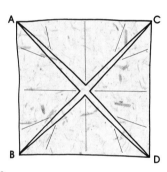

**9** This is the crease pattern.

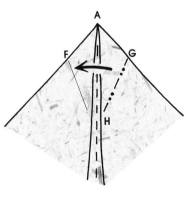

**10** The crease that runs to corner A should be a valley and the short crease from G to H, a mountain. If not, crease them . . .

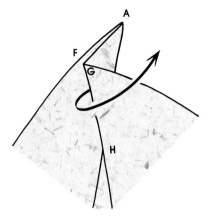

**11** . . . folding G across to F. Unfold.

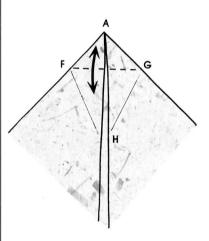

**12** Crease and unfold a valley fold between F and G.

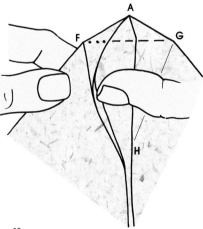

**13** Open up the paper on the left as shown, along the valley crease between F and H. Corner A will lift towards you.

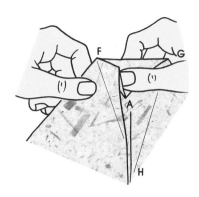

**14** Continue to open up the paper, letting A rise until it collapses down between the layers on the left, in an asymmetric way.

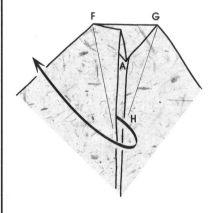

**15** Lift up the whole of the single layer of paper left of centre, but letting A remain collapsed down.

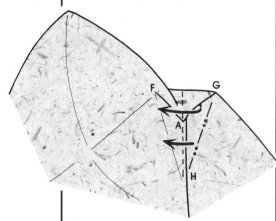

**16** As in Step 10, re-crease along AH and GH, bringing G across to F, on top of A.

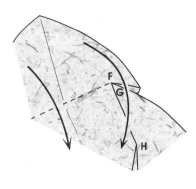

**17** Lower the single layer on the left back to its position in Step 15 but folding it down in front of G, trapping G between the layers.

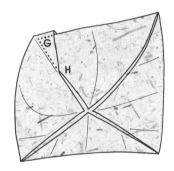

**18** This neatly locks the paper into a tight, slightly rounded corner. Repeat Steps 10–18 on the other three corners.

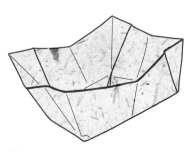

**19** The completed Egg Basket.

# HALLOWE'EN

★ ★ ★ ★ ★

# FANGS

*DESIGNED BY ERIC KENNEWAY, UK*

**T**his delightfully simple fold is great fun, and easily within the abilities of older children. Advanced folders could develop fangs which are longer and sharper – try experimenting.

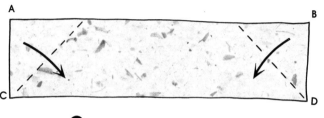

**1** Turn in corners A and B.

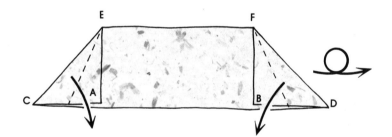

**2** Fold edge EC to lie along EA, and edge FD to lie along FB. Turn over.

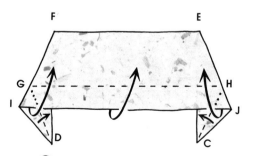

**3** Make crease GH, so that ID lies along DF and JC lies along CE . . .

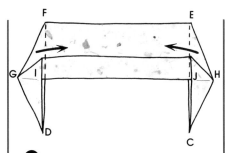

**4** . . . like this. Fold G and H towards the middle.

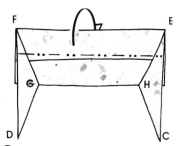
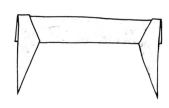

**5** Mountain fold FE behind to lie along GH.

**6** The completed Fangs.

# MAN IN THE MOON

*DESIGNED BY JOHN NORDQUIST, USA*

**T**his design looks very attractive on a greetings card or as a hanging decoration, suspended on a length of thread. Watch out, though – you must make the reverse folds very carefully or the proportions of the face will distort.

---

**STAR RATING ★★★**

**PAPERS**
Use a 15–25 cm (6–10 in) square of light- or mediumweight paper.

**OTHER EQUIPMENT**
To suspend the model you will need a needle and thread.

**SPECIAL NOTE**
Reverse folds (see Steps 6, 7 and 11) are explained in detail in the section on Folding Techniques (see Introduction).

---

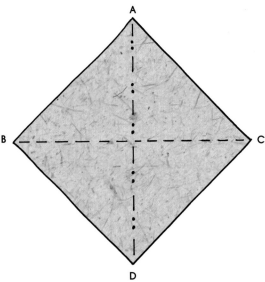

**❶** Crease BC as a valley and AD as a mountain. Unfold both.

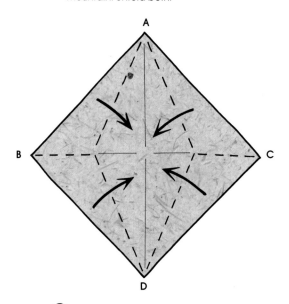

**❷** Fold edges AB and AC to crease AD, creasing down from A only as far as crease BC. Repeat on the bottom half, folding DB and DC to crease AD and creasing from D up as far as BC. Crease from this intersection to B and C, collapsing the paper . . .

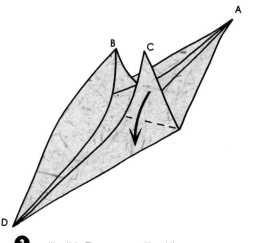

**3** . . . like this. The paper will not lie flat. Flatten C towards D.

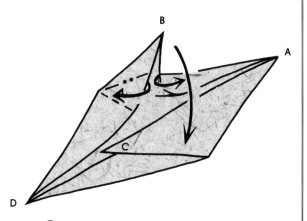

**4** Pull B open and squash flat . . .

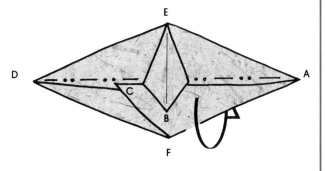

**5** . . . like this. Fold F behind to E. Rotate the paper to look like Step 6.

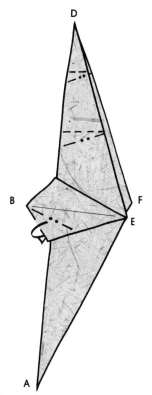

**6** Narrow B by folding behind as shown. Make two sets of crimp folds on the upper triangle as shown. The exact placement is important. Make the larger pair first, reverse folding along the mountain crease, then back along the valley. Repeat on the smaller pair.

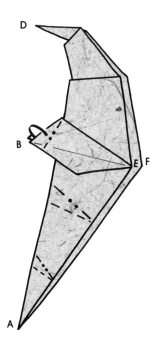

**7** Fold B behind as shown. Make two more sets of crimp folds on the lower triangle as described above, the larger set first.

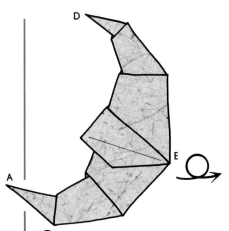

**8** The crimps complete. Turn over.

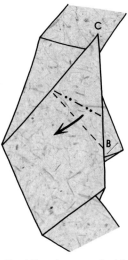

**9** Pleat C as shown, so that it creates . . .

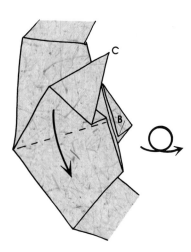

**10** . . . this shape. Fold C downwards. Turn over.

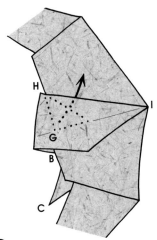

**11** Pull out corner G with a reverse fold, so that G becomes visible above edge HI.

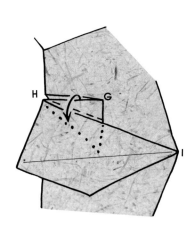

**12** Pull down the top layer of edge HG, partly squashing G open to form an eye . . .

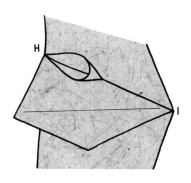

**13** . . . like this.

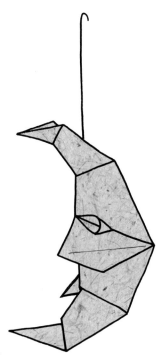

**14** The Man in the Moon complete. To suspend the model, attach a loop to the top with needle and thread.

# GHOST

## DESIGNED BY PAUL JACKSON, UK

**S**everal Ghosts, of varying sizes, could be suspended on a thread to decorate the home for Hallowe'en, or smaller ones can be used to decorate invitation cards to a 'Trick or Treat' party. The drawn eyes are a cheat, perhaps, but they do add a suitably ghoulish effect.

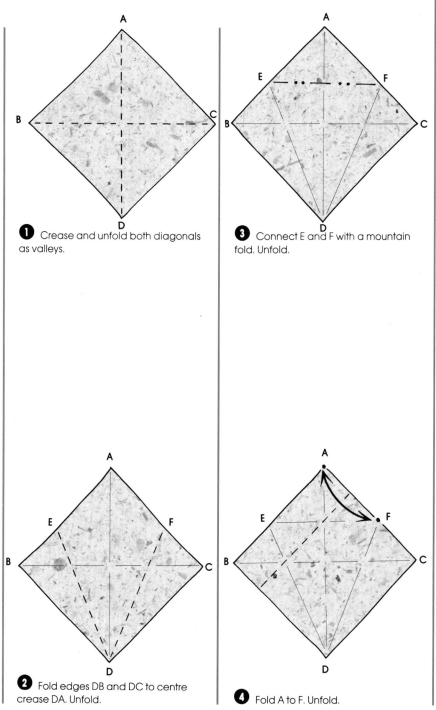

**STAR RATING** ★★★

**PAPERS**
Use a square of lightweight white paper; start with a sheet 15–20 cm (6–8 in) square.

**OTHER EQUIPMENT**
Marker pen; to suspend the ghost, you will need a needle and thread.

**1** Crease and unfold both diagonals as valleys.

**2** Fold edges DB and DC to centre crease DA. Unfold.

**3** Connect E and F with a mountain fold. Unfold.

**4** Fold A to F. Unfold.

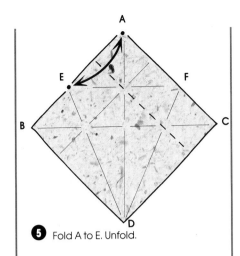

**5** Fold A to E. Unfold.

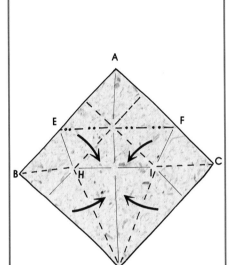

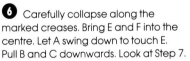

**6** Carefully collapse along the marked creases. Bring E and F into the centre. Let A swing down to touch E. Pull B and C downwards. Look at Step 7.

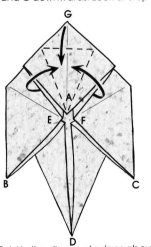

**7** Fold in the diagonal edges above EF to the centre crease, then fold down the top corner G on top.

**8** Unfold the side triangles, leaving the top corner folded down.

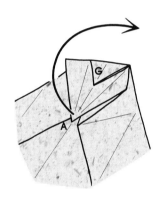

**9** Pick up the single layer corner A, and swivel it up and over the top edge of the paper . . .

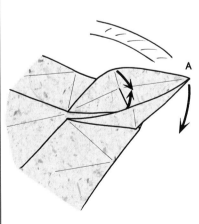

**10** . . . like this. The paper becomes 3-dimensional. Flatten corner A, allowing the sides to collapse inwards towards the centre crease.

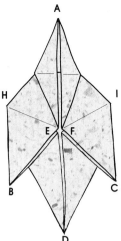

**11** The manoeuvre complete. Technically, the process shown in Steps 7–10 is known in origami as a petal fold.

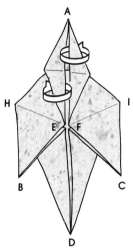

**12** Unfold AEF almost to a flat sheet, swinging edges AE and AF behind to touch G . . .

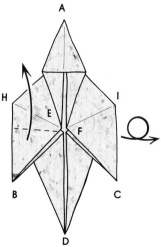

**13** . . . like this. Note the large triangle now below A. Fold up corner B. Turn over.

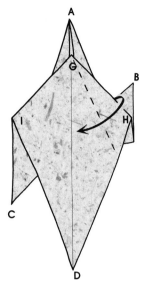

**14** Fold in edge GH, not quite as far as crease GD.

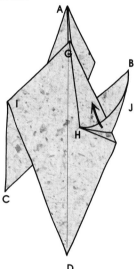

**15** Collapse flat the triangle between H and J . . .

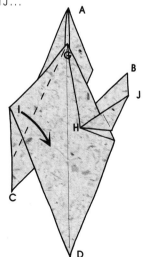

**16** . . . like this. Fold in edge GI, as shown.

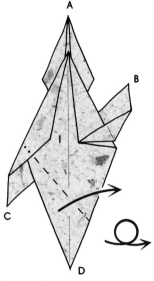

**17** Fold out D to the right. Turn over.

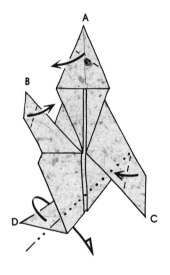

**18** Fold A out to the left. Fold in B and C. Pleat D downwards.

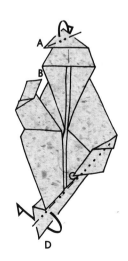

**19** Narrow A. Pleat D back upwards.

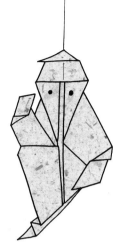

**20** The completed Ghost. Draw in the eyes as shown with a marker pen, and suspend using a needle and thread to attach a loop to the ghost's head.

# WITCH ON A BROOMSTICK

*DESIGNED BY PAUL JACKSON, UK*

**A**lthough simple in its final appearance, this model is tricky to fold. The secret is to make the early folds very accurate so that it collapses into shape without difficulty.

The Witch on a Broomstick is ideal for suspending from the ceiling. Make a whole coven to accompany a Man in the Moon (see page 98) and a haunting of Ghosts (see page 102) for a suitably eerie Hallowe'en celebration.

## STAR RATING ★★★★

### PAPERS
Use a 15–20 cm (6–8 in) square of lightweight paper which is white or coloured on one side and black on the reverse.

### OTHER EQUIPMENT
To suspend the model you will need a needle and thread.

### SPECIAL NOTE
Reverse folds (see Steps 7 and 8) are explained in detail in the section on Folding Techniques (see Introduction).

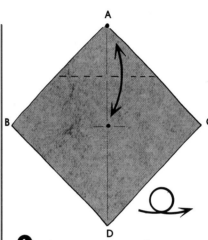

**1** Black side up, fold B to C, crease and unfold. Then fold A to D and pinch in the middle to find the centre point of the square – unfold. Fold A to the centre mark. Unfold. Turn over.

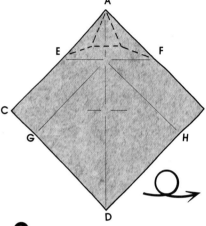

**3** Make five short, separate creases on triangle AFE. Turn over.

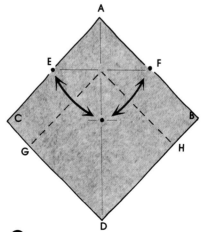

**2** White or coloured side up, fold E to the centre mark, creasing only from G to crease EF. Unfold. Repeat with F, creasing from H to crease EF. Unfold.

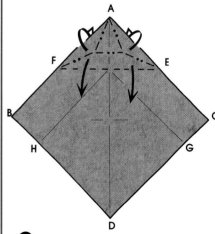

**4** Fold down crease FE, neatly collapsing all of the Step 5 creases . . .

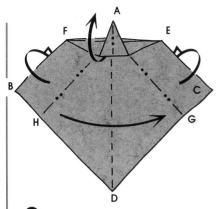

**5** ... like this. Collapse the paper in half by lifting the triangle below A, folding edges BF and CE behind and swinging H across to G. Look at Step 6.

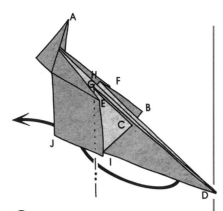

**8** Reverse fold D, so that the crease begins at G and is hidden behind the C flap. Edge GD reverses to touch corner J ...

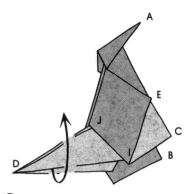

**11** Open out triangle D and view from below.

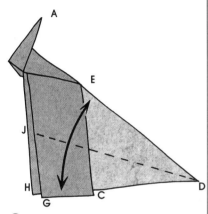

**6** Fold edge GD to edge ED. Unfold. Repeat behind.

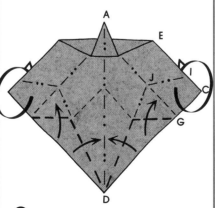

**9** ... like this. Turn the layers on triangle D completely inside out, so that the triangle (the broomstick) turns from black to white (or coloured). To do this open out the paper back to Step 5 ...

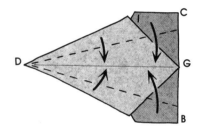

**12** Narrow triangle D, folding into the crease DG, taking B and C in with the white edge.

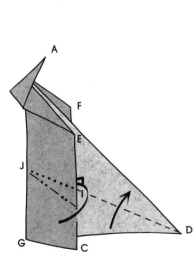

**7** Refold the Step 6 crease, but reversing the short crease JI to a mountain, pushing G up behind E. This is a reverse fold. Repeat behind.

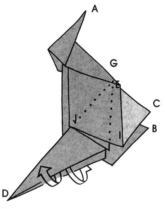

**10** ... like this. This diagram shows the pattern of creases. Refold the creases shown by a heavy dash from mountain to valley creases – all other creases remain the same. Collapse back to result in Step 11.

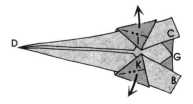

**13** Squash I and K ...

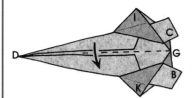

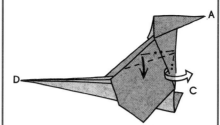

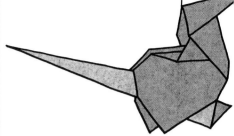

**14** . . . like this. Fold in half to resemble Step 10.

**15** Crimp across the body to form the arms, allowing the extra layer at the witch's spine to swivel backwards to create a hunched back.

**16** The completed Witch on a Broomstick. To suspend, attach a loop to the witch's hat (experiment to find the best position to balance the model) with a needle and thread.

# MASK

*DESIGNED BY PAUL JACKSON, UK*

**T**he problem when designing an origami mask is in creating holes for the eyes without resorting to scissors. One solution is to use a strip of paper for folding, as in this case. Using this strip-folding technique, many other mask designs can be created. Try some of your own and decorate to suit the occasion.

**STAR RATING ★★**

**PAPERS**
Use a strip of lightweight paper, proportioned 6:1; 60 x 10 cm (24 x 4 in) for adults and 42 x 7 cm (18 x 3 in) for children, are good average sizes.

**OTHER EQUIPMENT**
Sticky tape; length of cord elastic.

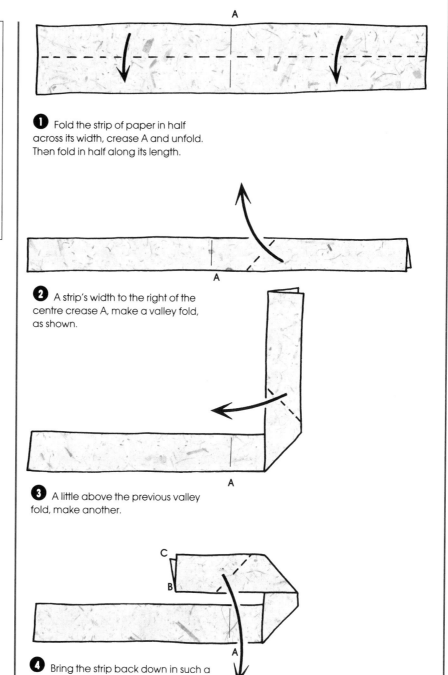

**1** Fold the strip of paper in half across its width, crease A and unfold. Then fold in half along its length.

**2** A strip's width to the right of the centre crease A, make a valley fold, as shown.

**3** A little above the previous valley fold, make another.

**4** Bring the strip back down in such a way that . . .

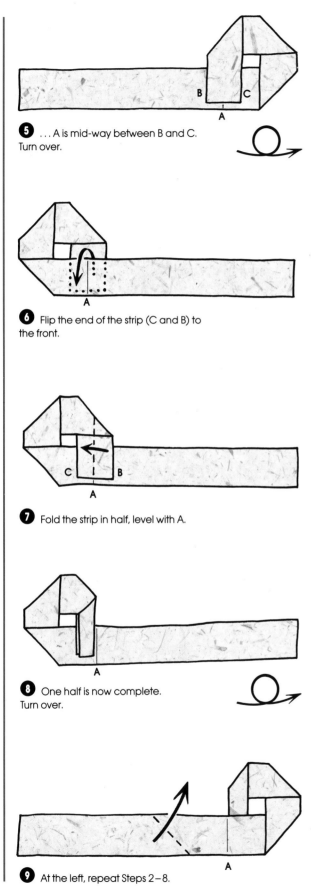

**5** ... A is mid-way between B and C. Turn over.

**6** Flip the end of the strip (C and B) to the front.

**7** Fold the strip in half, level with A.

**8** One half is now complete. Turn over.

**9** At the left, repeat Steps 2–8.

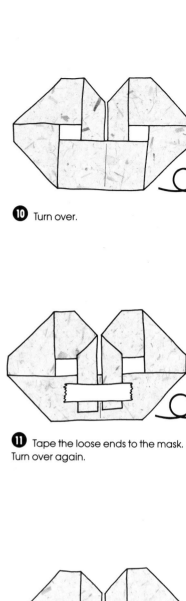

**10** Turn over.

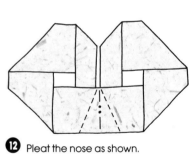

**11** Tape the loose ends to the mask. Turn over again.

**12** Pleat the nose as shown.

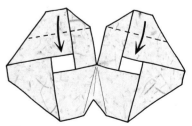

**13** Fold down the top edges, creating eyebrows.

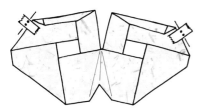

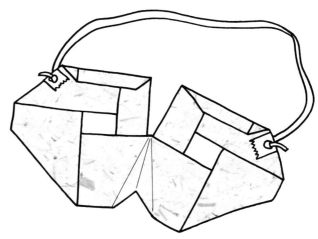

**14** Add sticky tape as shown. To create enough strength to hold the elastic without tearing, tape a few layers over each other. Pierce the tape and feed the elastic through. Tie the ends to the mask, leaving enough elastic between the knots to hold the mask to your head.

**15** The completed Mask.

# 6

# GIFTS

★ ★ ★ ★ ★

# STANDING HEART

### DESIGNED BY PAUL JACKSON, UK

**A** Valentine's Day design for the practical romantics among us, this free-standing heart is durable enough to last for months displayed on a table or shelf – maybe even until the Buttonhole (see page 123) arrives the following year . . .

**STAR RATING ★★★**

**PAPERS**
You will need a 15–20 cm (6–8 in) square of light- or mediumweight paper which is white on one side and red on the other.

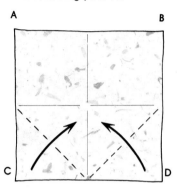

**1** White side up, fold the square in half, horizontally and vertically. Unfold. Fold C and D to the centre.

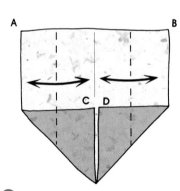

**2** Fold A and B to the centre crease. Unfold.

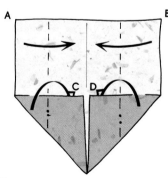

**3** Refold along the Step 2 creases, but reverse folding the coloured triangles behind C and D . . .

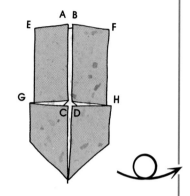

**4** . . . like this. Turn over.

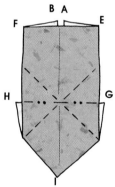

**5** Pre-crease as shown. Note that GH is a mountain crease.

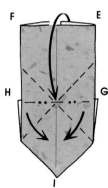

**6** Collapse so that edge FE drops to be level with corner I.

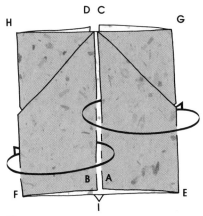

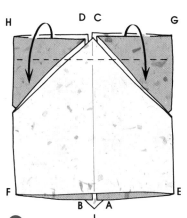

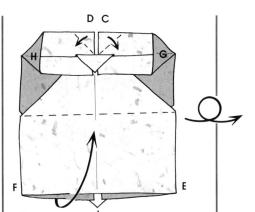

**7** Open the central slit and fold B and then A behind edge FE, so that the new top layer becomes white. To do this, unfold the paper almost back to Step 1, then re-crease and collapse back to Step 8.

**8** Pull down edge HG as shown and squash flat the triangles at H and G . . .

**9** . . . like this. Turn in D and C. Lift edge FE along a horizontal crease mid-way up the paper, separating FE from I and providing a back edge to support the heart when it is stood up. Turn over.

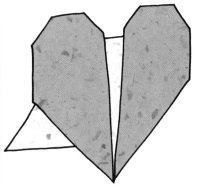

**10** The completed Standing Heart.

# GIFT ENVELOPE

## *TRADITIONAL*

**T**his envelope should not be mailed, but it is an attractive and creative way to present a card delivered by hand.

**STAR RATING ★★**

**PAPERS**

Use lightweight paper, preferably textured, patterned or hand-decorated.

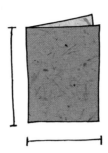

**1** Measure the greetings card.

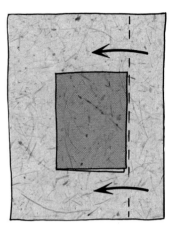

**3** Place the card approximately in the centre of the paper, square to the edges. Fold in the right-hand edge.

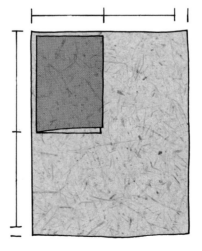

**2** Put the card into a corner of the envelope paper. Measure twice the height and twice the width of the card on the paper, then add a little extra. Trim the paper to these dimensions.

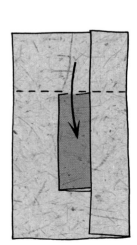

**4** Fold down the top edge.

**OPPOSITE** Gift envelopes in an array of sizes, shapes and colours add a special touch to hand-delivered greetings cards for all occasions. See overleaf for the continuing instructions for this project.

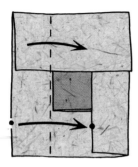

**5** Fold in the left edge, as shown.

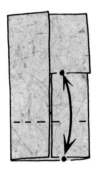

**6** Fold and unfold the bottom edge, as shown.

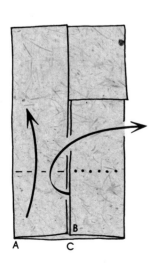

**7** Valley fold A up the left-hand edge. Open B . . .

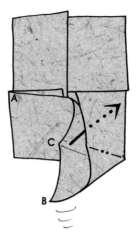

**8** . . . and push C deep inside, making a mountain fold across the bottom.

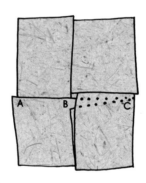

**9** The completed Gift Envelope.

# VARIATION

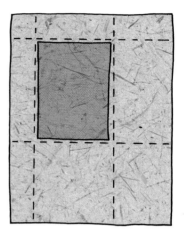

**1** The card can be placed anywhere on the paper at Step 3, even right up into a corner, as shown.

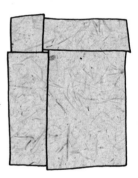

**2** Follow the steps as before to achieve this off-centre look.

# GIFT BOXES

*DESIGNED BY PAUL JACKSON, UK*

**A**ll the lids in these examples are locked using the same twist technique, but a change in the angle of twist can create surprisingly diverse results. Both lids and boxes must be constructed with great accuracy so that all the edges are parallel, the angles are equal and the creases are placed with care. Take your time if you want a really professional result.

## LID

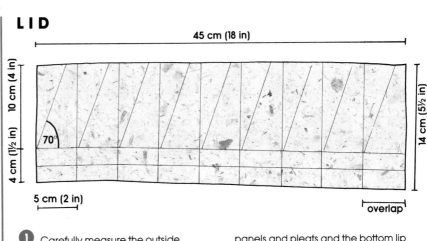

**①** Carefully measure the outside dimensions of the lid (45 x 14 cm/18 x 5½ in) and cut out the lid as shown. Draw in the positions of the nine panels and pleats and the bottom lip using the measurements shown. The critical angle of 70° should be accurately made for each pleat.

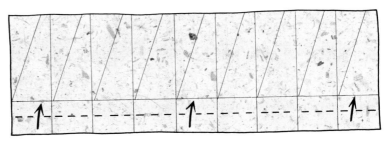

**②** Fold up along the bottom crease.

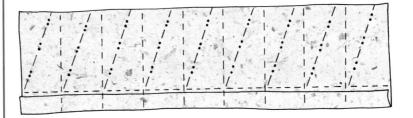

**③** Crease mountains and valleys as shown.

119

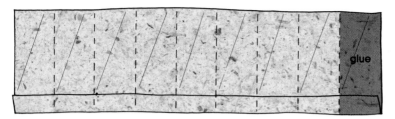

**4** Reinforce the vertical creases. Apply glue to the right end panel, and then join it to the back of the left end panel. This will create an eight-sided sleeve.

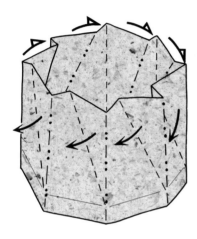

**5** Carefully pleat mountains and valleys as shown. For Step 6 to form, *all* ceases must form at the same time and interlock equally around the middle. It may take a little time to wriggle all the pleats into place, but it will help if the bottom edge is kept as close to a perfect octagon as possible. If it goes out of shape, the locking will become more difficult.

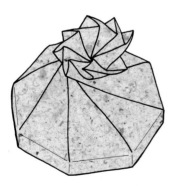

**6** The lid complete.

# BOX

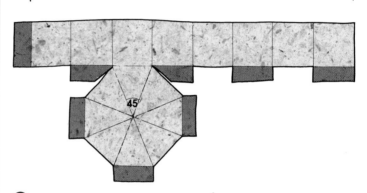

**1** Measure out the box paper as shown, so that the panels are fractionally narrower than the lid panels. In this way, the lid will fit snugly over the box. Construct the octagonal using a protractor to measure the angles (see Tip – Making Boxes). Apply glue to the tabs and fold the box into shape.

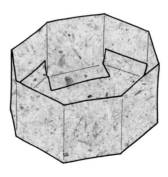

**2** The completed box. The lid will fit on top.

**OPPOSITE** The completed eight-side gift box (right). To make six-sided and five-sided boxes (left and centre) with flat lids, see the instructions overleaf.

# FLAT LIDS

### EIGHT-SIDED

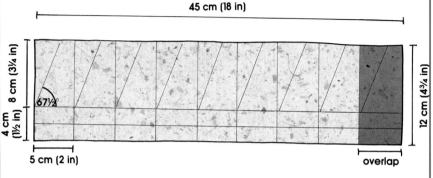

**45 cm (18 in)**

**8 cm (3¼ in)**

**4 cm (1½ in)**

**67½°**

**12 cm (4¾ in)**

**5 cm (2 in)**

**overlap**

**1** The lid on the first drawing had a 70° angle. This caused the locking point to rise above the level of the lid, creating a pyramid effect. If you reduce the angle to 67½°, the lock will be level with the top of the lid and so the lid will be flat. In all other respects, make the lid as before.

### SIX-SIDED

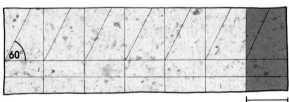

**60°**

**overlap**

**2** A 60° angle with seven panels (one to overlap) will create a flat six-sided lid. The box piece must also, of course, be six-sided, with an hexagonal base (see Tip – Making Boxes).

### FIVE-SIDED

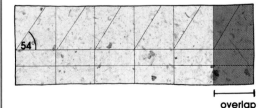

**54°**

**overlap**

**3** Similarly, a 54° angle with six panels will create a flat five-sided lid.

# BUTTONHOLE

*LEAF: DESIGNED BY ALICE GRAY, US*
*FLOWER: TRADITIONAL JAPANESE*

**T**his is a beautiful design that will make a much admired gift, particularly if the papers are chosen with care. The flower is the Iris from the Floral Centrepiece (see page 70).

**STAR RATING ★★★**

**PAPERS**

The **leaf** and the **flower** are each made from a 10 cm (4 in) square of lightweight paper (such as origami paper). These dimensions will make quite a small buttonhole, so fold with care.

The **stem** is made from a square of lightweight paper, half the size of that used for the flower or leaf, and trimmed to a 3:1 rectangle.

## LEAF

**1** Form a centre crease between two points and unfold. Fold the top edges to the centre crease.

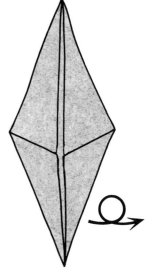

**3** Turn over.

**2** Fold the bottom edges to the centre crease.

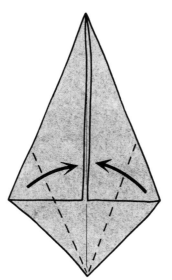

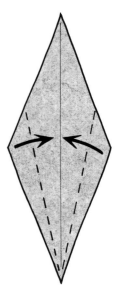

**4** Fold the bottom edges to the centre crease.

## FLOWER

See Floral Centrepiece (page 70) and follow the instructions for the Iris to complete the flower.

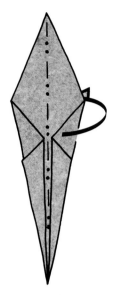

**5** Mountain fold the right half behind the left half.

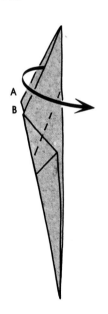

**6** Fold the front layer B across to the right. A and B will separate.

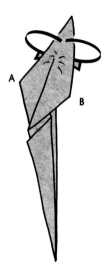

**7** Invert the leaf from a concave shape to a convex one.

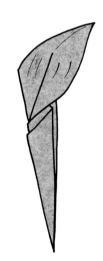

**8** The completed leaf.

## ASSEMBLY

**1** With your tongue, wet the bottom of the flower to soften the paper. Push the stem through the wet paper, so that the rolled end catches deep inside the bloom preventing the stem from falling right through.

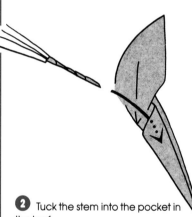

**2** Tuck the stem into the pocket in the leaf.

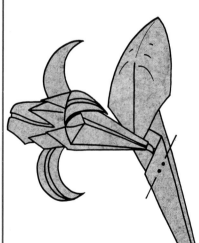

**3** The completed Buttonhole. A better shape may be achieved if a mountain fold is made where shown.

## STEM

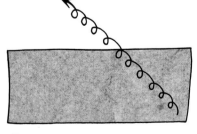

**1** Roll up the paper for the stem as tightly as possible.

**2** At the loose end, roll over the tip to lock the tube.

**3** The stem complete.

# INDEX

# ACKNOWLEDGEMENTS

The author would like to thank the following for permission to publish their designs: Dave Brill, Alice Gray, John N Nordquist and Ed Sullivan.

The *Fangs* and *Man in the Moon* were first published in the monthly origami magazine *The Flapping Bird*, edited by Sam Randlett and published by Jay Marshall, Chicago, US, between 1968 and 1976. The *Bauble* is by an unknown author, possibly in the US: further information would be gratefully received. The head section of the *Easter Bunny* was first published in *Paper Magic* by Robert Harbin, published by Oldbourne, UK, 1956.

# ORIGAMI SOCIETIES

If you have enjoyed folding the designs in *Festive Folding*, you may like to join an organized club of paper folders. The three listed here cater well for the beginner and have many overseas members. The first two listed also publish a magazine and sell origami books and papers:

British Origami Society
253 Park Lane
Poynton
Stockport
Cheshire SK12 1RH
England

The Friends of the Origami Center of America
15 West 77th Street
New York
NY 10024
USA

New Zealand Origami Society
79 Dunbar Road
Christchurch 3
New Zealand